By

Disclaimer

The information provided in this book is designed to provide helpful information on the subjects discussed. The author's books are only meant to provide the reader with the basics knowledge of a certain topic, without any warranties regarding whether the student will, or will not, be able to incorporate and apply all the information provided. Although the writer will make his best effort share his insights, learning is a difficult task and each person needs a different timeframe to fully incorporate a new topic. This book, nor any of the author's books constitute a promise that the reader will learn a certain topic within a certain timeframe.

LEARN C++ IN A DAY
The Ultimate Crash Course to Learning the Basics of C++ in No Time

Table of Contents

Chapter 1: An Introduction

Objective: Get a brief introduction, history, and understanding of the C++ language.

C++ is widely known as a low-level, advanced language that every programmer should know. One main difference between C and C++ is object-oriented programming (OOP). The OOP side of C++ is probably makes it much more difficult to understand and learn. This ebook is meant to help new programmers with the language, including help with OOP methodologies and structures.

A Brief History of C++

The C++ language first appeared in the 1980s. It was created by a Danish computer scientist named Bjarne Stroustrup. The original name for the language was "C with Classes," but was later changed to C++. The main original purpose for C++ was adding OOP to the older C language.

As the years went on, C++ evolved and was standardized. C++ was created as a low-level language, which means that it works closes to binary level programming. As a matter of fact, the language was originally created to work only one step above binary or assembly language. The closer a language is to actual machine language makes it faster and more flexible with low-level machine manipulation such as memory processing and storage.

What is C++ Used For?

The single most basic reason developers still use a language that's over 30 years old is performance. Remember that languages that are closer to the binary computer language are always faster than bulky overhead languages such as Java, C# or VB. The latter three languages still have their uses, but C++ is mostly used for programming where alternative languages are unable to fully cover aspects of development.

As a new developer, the world is your horizon and you can use any language you want. However, there are some industries where you won't be able to use any language other than C++. The C++ language is engrained in several areas of IT and software development.

Gaming is probably the number one area of IT where you'll need to know C++. C++ is used to create gaming engines. Other languages are too bulky and waste resources. Since gaming engines are concerned with speed and quality of rendering, C++ is the language used for low-level programming in gaming design. It's usually coded along with other languages in gaming design, so it helps a developer to understand multiple languages when getting into game programming.

Device drivers are almost exclusively done in C++. C is used in embedded systems, but the drivers used to integrate hardware with larger systems such as desktops, servers and mobile devices are all coded with C++. Device drivers are the software programs used to allow the hardware component to work with an operating system. Device drivers are specific to the operating system, but C++ works across any platform. Device driver writers use C++ for its speed and platform-independent integration. Once compiled, the program is specific to the operating system, but you can use C++ to write for Linux, Windows, and Apple systems.

Imaging and video processing software uses C++. It's again used for its speed. It can take days to render an image or video with slow hardware and software. C++ overcomes much of the bulky overhead of other languages. Similar to gaming development, the imaging and video rendering industries also prefer C++.

The telecom and networking industries use C++ to code the hardware necessary for communication. Routers, voice systems such as PBXes, hubs, and switches use C++ as the backend coding language. Network engineers usually have a firm grasp of the C++ language, especially those who build hardware systems.

Finally, we mentioned C is used in embedded systems, which is the standard. However, some embedded system designs use C++ instead. C++ has a bit more overhead than its predecessor C, so it's not usually preferred. But C++ offers more options and libraries than C, so it's needed in more complex systems.

Financial systems and analysis rely heavily on C++ for its speed and precision. If you play the stock market, you're relying on systems and number crunching controlled by C++ programming.

Why Use C++?

Most new programmers are confused between the differences of C++ and C. They don't know when to use the C++ language over C, or any language for that matter.

The main difference with C++ is its use of object-oriented programming. This isn't capable with the C language. This does not make the C language inferior, it just makes C++ accessible to additional libraries and coding possibilities.

With object-oriented programming, you can use constructors and destructors. A constructor instantiates the class and a destructor removes it from memory. We'll learn about these concepts in future chapters.

Java developers sometimes switch to C++ programming. Java is a language similar to C++ but it's a much higher level language that isn't compiled. Java is an interpreter that runs on any platform, but it can be much slower than the C++ language.

Overall, the main reason to use C++ is for speed. If you ever want to get into very low-level, fast coding that handles memory functions much more efficiently, you want to use C++. This ebook attempts to give a new programmer and introduction to the language.

What You Need to Code in C++

C++ is a compiled language, which means that you need a compiler before you can complete the coding process. You could type the code in a regular text file, but it's not recommended and you'll still need a compiler even if you do write perfect code with no errors. Remember that compiled languages depend on the operating system on which they are compiled. This means that if you compile your code on a Windows machine, the software will only work with Windows. You'll need to code your program on another operating system for it to work on a different system.

A simple Google search will help you find a compiler that suits you. Some compilers are made for both Linux and Windows. Others work on only one platform. Once you choose your compiler, you need to store it in a directory on your machine.

You also need an IDE. The IDE is what you code in. It gives you the color coded text interface that helps you write better code. The color coded text lets you quickly identify data types, comments, classes, and other common code structures. In other words, it makes it easier to read. Most compilers come with an IDE, so check this out before you install the IDE.

Once you determine which compiler and IDE that you want to use, you then need to install it on your system. The IDE should have an EXE or MSI package for you to just automatically install the software without using any command lines. If you're using a Linux based system, you probably need some extra configurations.

After you install the software, open the compiler to get a feel for how it works. You'll be working directly in the C++ IDE, so get a feel for the color coding. For instance, comments are usually displayed in green text. A data type is set in a blue color. Classes are color coded in blue as well. Strings are either red or blue. Standard variables including your function names are in black.

At the bottom of the IDE, you'll see the build log and debugger. These are two windows that are most important for your programming success. The build log tells you if any errors occurred when the C++ compiler created the executable, compiled program. The debugger is used when you want to step through the code and identify which part of the code is causing you errors.

Some IDEs have a "to do" list. A to do list is a set of code blocks set with TODO in the comments. This tells the coder that he needs to work more with the code, and he's not finished.

If the IDE developer is kind, you start with a temporary Hello World program when you first run the program. This can be compiled and displayed in the console, so you can see the way the compiler and the language work. Also note that C++ coding files end with the .cpp file extension. This is important when you're searching your hard drive for the necessary coding files for your program.

What You'll Learn in This EBook

The goal for us is to get you acclimated as a new programmer in C++. C++ is a massive language, but you can take the beginning concepts and turn into an advanced programmer with some practice. We're giving you the toolset, and you can use it to work with the more complex procedures.

In the first lesson, we'll introduce you to the basics of C++. You'll need to know the basic structures and programming concepts before you begin actual coding.

Next, we'll give you an introduction to variable data types and what you can do to call certain variables. Variables are used in any programming language, so once you learn one language, you'll easily learn any others.

Next, we'll learn about operators and how to perform arithmetic with your C++ programs. We then get into advanced data types, and what you can do to convert from one data type to another. We also introduce you to the string class, which is different from the primitive string or character data type.

We then go into the loops and conditional programming structures. These are also very popular in any programming language. Loops and conditional statements control the way a program executes.

Getting a little more complex, we then get into arrays. Arrays are a bit more complex, but they are necessary in any language. Even low level languages such as C use arrays intensely.

One of the most difficult parts to learn in the C+ language is object-oriented programming. OOP is much different than standard linear languages. OOP creates components out of your code, so you can code in a compartmental fashion.

With OOP, you need to know inheritance, which is the concept of using parent structures for reusable code. Inheritance is another common OOP concept.

Once you work through this eBook, you should have all the necessary tools to code in C++ including an understanding of how the language works.

Lab Questions

1. What type of code is constructed with the C++ language?

a. Compiled
b. Interpreted
c. Plain text
d. Binary

Explanation: C++ is a compiled language, so the C++ compiler takes the plain text code you create and turns it into binary files.

2. What is the interface called that color codes your C++ text for easier reading and coding?

a. Compiler
b. Interpreter

c. IDE
d. TODO list

Explanation: The IDE is the window where you construct your code. It organizes your files, shows you the debugger, and keeps your TODO list.

3. What is one industry that always uses C++ for its engines?

a. Healthcare
b. IT
c. Gaming
d. Development

Explanation: The gaming industry uses C++ to make fast gaming engines that render images and video quickly.

4. What is the main reason you would use C++ over other languages such as Java or C#?

a. Less code needed
b. Performance and speed
c. Easier to learn
d. Used more often

Explanation: C++ is closer to binary language than other high-level languages, so it's much faster and speeds up code execution.

5. If you were going to code an embedded system, what is the most likely language you'd use?

a. C
b. C++
c. Java
d. C#

Explanation: The C++ language is useful for several industries, but embedded systems still need small programs that aren't too resource intensive. C is the main language for embedded systems.

6. What software turns your C++ code into a readable executable for your computer?

a. Compiler
b. Interpreter
c. Command line
d. MSI packages

Explanation: The compiler is responsible for turning your C++ into binaries, which are the code instructions for your computer to execute.

Chapter 2: C++ Basics

Objective: This chapter gives you a brief yet good overview of C++ basics that every programmer must know to get started with the language.

Before you start any language, it's important to understand some of the basics. Luckily, coding basics are usually the same across several languages, which make it easy to learn more coding structures as you move on from C++. Once you understand basic C++ concepts, you can take these concepts and apply them towards other languages. Many newer languages are based on C-style coding, so you have an advantage as a new C++ learner.

Program Structure and Comments

The best way to understand the basics is to take a look at a basic program. Let's look at a basic program that sends output to the display that says "Hello World."

```
// my first program in C++
#include <iostream>

int main()
{
  std::cout << "Hello World!";
  return 0;
}
```

Notice that we have a specific format for each line of code. The comments are the first line of code.

The double slash (//) character indicates to the compiler that you want to include a comment. Comments are completely ignored by the processor, so you can write whatever you want in this section. You can also use multi-lined comments in C++. Here is an example using the same code above.

```
/* I
can code in
C++ */
#include <iostream>

int main()
{
  std::cout << "Hello World!";
  return 0;
}
```

Any content within the slashes and asterisks is ignored when the compiler creates your program. When you type comments in the IDE, they will usually color code as green. When you only have one line of comments, it's standard to use the // comment indicator. When you have multiple lines, use the /* */ comment architecture.

Next you see the include statement. This is the way you include other libraries. C++ code files need a way to integrate with other files. Your programs won't be one long page. They will be separate, distinct pages. You can have classes and functions organized into hundreds of files in a program. The way you integrate them is include them as libraries. In this example, the included library is iostream. The brackets indicate that it's an internal C++ library. Custom coded libraries are included in quotes, and you'll see the .h file extension for header files. We'll get into header files and includes in later chapters.

The next statement starts the main function. The main function is the one, central point where execution begins. Think of the main function as the starting point like a front door. When you visit a building, you don't know where to go or where your destination office is located. To figure it out, you go through the front door, look at a directory, and then travel to your office. The same is true for the C++ language and compiled programs.

C++ searches your code for the main function. From this function, you branch out to difference sections of your code and instruct the compiler on how it should execute its code. Without the main function, the compiler would not know where to start. Therefore, you'll always see a main function in a C++ program.

You'll notice the "int" statement prior to the main function name. The main function always returns an integer. When the main function returns 0, it means that no errors were found during execution. Any other number returned indicates that there was an error, so your program stopped unnaturally with errors.

Within the main function brackets is the main code for your program. In this example, we only have one line of code. We display "Hello World" to the default display. In most systems, the default display is the monitor. The "<<" characters indicate that you want to send output to the display.

Brackets are always used to organize a program's code. They are used in loops and conditional statements. They are also used with functions, as you can see from the previous code.

When you compile the above code, you see "Hello World" on your screen. That's all it takes to create your first C++ program.

Functions and Return Values

We'll get more heavily into functions in chapter 8, but you must know the basics of a function before you can write the code.

Let's return to the Hello World example.

```cpp
// my first program in C++
#include <iostream>

int main()
{
  std::cout << "Hello World!";
  return 0;
}
```

We explained this small program in the previous section, but we're going to focus on the function section this time.

A function always starts with a data type that's return. You can also return no data. Functions that don't return any value are giving the void data type. Void functions are similar to subroutines. They perform an action and even sometimes display information to the user, but no return value is sent to the calling statement.

After the data type declaration, the function is given a name. This can be any name as long as it's not a reserved C++ keyword. The open and close parenthesis indicates the area where arguments are sent to the function. You can also send no arguments to the function. As with the main function in our example, no parameters are set for the function, so it's just an open and close set of parenthesis with nothing contained.

All statements within a function are enclosed with the open and closing brackets. If you left them out, the compiler would not know where one function began and the next ended. This can be difficult when you use brackets with loops and conditional statements. Make sure you format your code so finding missing brackets is easy. Notice that we've tabbed the statements over, so the closing bracket is aligned with the ending one. This type of formatting is standard in the coding industry, because it makes your code much easier to read.

The final part of a function is always the return statement. You only need a return when the function indicates that a return value is needed. In the case of this function, we indicate that the function returns an integer. Therefore, the return statement returns 0. Since 0 means that the program executed normally, this tells the compiler that the program executed without errors.

When you work with C++, you'll have several functions with return values and void data types. If you forget to return a value when the function indicates one is returned, the compiler displays an error.

Variables

Variables are the containers for your values whether they are numbers, characters, or other data types. Variables hold any data that you need to manipulate and output to your users.

Let's take a look at a simple numeric variable.

int mynumber = 5;

In this example, we create a variable named mynumber. Notice the first part of the statement is "int." This indicates to the compiler that you want an integer created.

The format of a variable declaration is always the data type and then the variable name. The following format is what you'll always use to create a variable.

datatype variable;

Notice that a semicolon is always at the end of the variable declaration even in the template. The semicolon is what tells the compiler that the end of a statement has been found. You can place your code in multiple lines on the IDE as long as you indicate to the compiler when the statement should terminate. Let's look at an example of a statement that uses multiple IDE lines but still indicates the end using a semicolon.

int
mynumber = 5;

We added a carriage return after the int statement. Even though there is a carriage return, the compiler continues reading as if the statement continues. Once it meets with the semicolon character, it knows to stop the statement. If you forget a semicolon in your statements, you will receive an error during compiling, because the compiler doesn't know when to stop the current statement and begin with a new one. This leads to a syntax error.

It can be difficult to find a missing semicolon in several lines of code, so ensure that you keep track of your statements and always end them with a semicolon. Forgetting a semicolon is one of a coder's biggest headaches.

Your variable names should always be descriptive and explain your values. For instance, you wouldn't name a variable "cow" when it's used to hold a breed of horses.

When you give your variables descriptive names that help identify the values stored, it's much easier to read the code and debug it if you have issues later.

You also can't use special characters, spaces or punctuation in your variable names. Variable names must start with an underscore or a number. Any deviation from this naming scheme and the compiler gives you an error.

The main rules to remember when creating a variable is to give them a name that matches the values they contain, and you must use the right starting character. Most developers use letters or an underscore to define their variables. Some use a prefix that indicates the data type as the code continues. For example:

int intMynumber = 5;

This standard isn't as popular anymore, but it's still used in some applications. The theory is that it's easier to read when you debug statements several lines after you've defined the data type. This variable naming scheme tells you instantly what type of variable is defined and what data it can hold.

Operators

Operators are the operations you make on your variables. We'll get more detailed in chapter 4, but it's good to have a brief overview of operators.

Operators can be mathematical, assignments, incremental and decremental, and comparisons. There are numerous operators in C++, and we'll go over them in more detail in chapter 4. Here are the basics.

The very basic operator is the equal sign. The equal sign is what assigns a value to a variable. After you set up your variable, you then assign it a value. In the previous section, we did assignment and declaration of a variable in one line of code, but you can separate them.

Using the above mynumber variable, let's separate assignment and declaration.

```
int mynumber;
mynumber = 5;
```

In the above block of code, we've first declared the variable. Remember that you always need to declare a variable before you can use it. C++ requires explicit variable assignment unlike other languages such as Python. You also need to give it a data type unlike Python. Once you define a variable, the operating system allocates memory for it.

Since the compiler knows that the variable is an integer, it knows the amount of space to allocate. In this example, we use the equal sign operator to tell the compiler to store the number five in the variable mynumber. Again, we terminate the statement with the semicolon.

The main operators you'll work with are arithmetic. Let's take a look at a math operator.

```
int mynumber;
int mynumber = 5+5;
```

In this statement, we used the plus sign operator, or addition. C++ includes all mathematical operators including addition, subtraction, multiplication, division, and modulation. Modulo returns the remainder of a division statement.

You can also use mathematical operators on variables and store them in a second variable. Let's take a look at an example.

```
int mynumber;
int mynewnumber;
mynumber = 5;
mynewnumber = mynumber + 5;
```

In the above code, we create two variables. We then assign the original mynumber variable to the value of 5. We then want to add 5 to that number, but we don't want to override the existing variable value. We use the second variable to hold the result of the addition calculation. This is beneficial when you want to create a temporary variable to contain an original value while you perform calculations on a new mathematical process. The temporary variable contains the original value, and the result of the calculation is contained in another. You can then perform a comparison on the original and the new variable.

This chapter went over some of the very basic functionalities in C++, but they are extremely important to understand. You'll use these concepts in even very basic programs to very complex programs. What's great about learning these concepts is that they can be applied to other languages, which makes this learning experience double beneficial for new programmers.

Lab Questions

1. What is the function name that every C++ program contains as the entry point for code execution?

a. main
b. enter

c. begin

d. out

Explanation: The main function is the starting point for all C and C++ programs. Your programs must contain a main function to execute.

2. What is the return type of any main function in a C++ program?

a. string

b. character

c. integer

d. decimal

Explanation: The main function returns an integer value. If the program runs without issues, a return type of 0 is sent back to the calling process, which indicates no errors occurred.

3. What is always at the beginning of a variable declaration statement?

a. the value

b. the variable name

c. a semicolon

d. the data type

Explanation: The data type tells the operating system what type of value is contained, so the right memory allocation can be made.

4. What operator is used to assign a value to a variable?

a. =

b. +

c. ==

d. –

Explanation: The equal sign is used to assign a value on the right side of the statement to the variable name on the left side. The == is also a valid operator, but it's a comparison operator, which would cause a standard assigned statement to fail during execution.

Chapter 3: Variables and Data Types

Objective: This chapter covers variables and data types that we highlighted in the previous chapter. We will get more in depth and in detail for these C++ structures.

We just covered the surface in the last chapters when it comes to variables and data types. You need much more information to get started programming in C++. Variables are the main foundation for a program, so you should have a deep understanding before you get started programming. Data types define these variables, so you'll need to learn these concepts together as they go hand-in-hand during the coding process.

Memory Addresses

Before we get into creating variables and data types, we first need to understand how the computer assigns variables in memory. This will give us a better understanding of the reason we need to define a data type and the way these values are allocated in memory.

The smallest unit of memory is called a bit. A bit is either a one or a zero. Since we need more than just a one or a zero to perform coding instructions, memory is laid out with several memory units' side-by-side. These memory units are a byte. The smallest amount of memory that you can allocate is a byte, which is comprised of 8 bits.

A data type tells the compiler and the operating system what type of data is stored in these memory address spaces, and it tells them how it should be interpreted. It's the CPU that's responsible for translating your coding instructions into binary and storing them in memory. When you make a call to retrieve the value, the CPU finds the memory location and sends it back to your code.

The data type tells the compiler the amount of memory that should be allocated and set aside for the variable value. An integer only needs a byte of memory space, but a string or an array might need much more memory space. If you try to store a string in a variable that was defined as an integer, the compiler would throw an error and memory allocation would fail because not enough memory was set aside. This is why it's important to know the type of variable you need before you define a function or procedure.

Defining Numeric Variables

There are two types of numeric variables in C++. The first is the integer. We've seen several snippets of code using an integer, so you should be somewhat familiar with these data types. An integer is a whole number. It can be a negative or positive whole number, but what you should remember is that there is never a decimal value with an integer.

The next type of variable is a decimal or float value. The decimal data type is available in some languages, but C++ refers to a decimal variable as a float. The decimal number can have a 0 in the decimal place, but it always has a fraction as part of the value. Float data types can also be negative or positive.

Let's take a look at some examples. First let's review integers again.

```
int mynumber = 5;
```

We discussed this assignment in the last chapter. The int data type is first used, and then we define the variable name. We don't always need to initialize the variable with a value. Sometimes, we don't know the value that we want to use until later in the program. The following syntax is also valid.

```
int mynumber;
mynumber = 5;
```

The second line of code can be after the variable initialization or several lines below it. This lets you assign a value when you don't have a value for it until later in the program.

You can also assign multiple variables in the same line of code. Let's take a look at multiple initialization.

```
int mynumber = 5, anothernumber = 10;
```

Notice that the second number doesn't have a data type indicated. This is shorthand when you need to define several variables with multiple data types. Suppose you want to define multiple variables but don't know the value. The following code lets you initialize a variable without assigning a value.

```
int mynumber, anothernumber;
```

Both variables are set as integers. Note that you must be uniform when you create variables. You can mix initialization types. The following syntax is invalid and throws an error in your code.

```
int mynumber, anothernumber = 5;
```

These examples show you integer numbers, but we could also use this same syntax for decimal or floating point numbers. Let's take a look at the same code except with a floating point data type.

float mynumber = 5.5, anothernumber = 10.5;

We've used shorthand again to reassign the same variables with a float data type. We also changed the numeric values to floating point values. We could assign a float integer with a whole integer number, but then later change the value to a decimal. As long as you define a variable as a floating point decimal, you can assign it a decimal value at any time.

One thing to note about the change of variable assignment: you cannot create a new variable with the same name as another variable. We assume that we wanted to reassign the data type of the original variable, but if we added this to the original integer assignment code, the compiler would give us an error. For instance, the following code would give us an error.

float mynumber = 5.5, anothernumber = 10.5;
int mynumber = 5, anothernumber = 10;

In other words, all variables within scope (we will define scope later) must have a different name.

Characters and Strings

We keep showing examples of numbers and integers as examples, because numeric values are the simplest variables and values to understand. However, a big part of your programming experience will be in using and manipulating string variables. String variables are the "words" in a program.

They prompt users and allow users to store strings as values such as their name and address.

Since C++ is derived from C, the first important point to note is that a word or a string is an array of characters. C has no library for strings, so you must work with character arrays. C++ has a string library, so you can work with strings in the same way you work with them in other languages.

Let's first look at the char data type, so you can understand characters and how they are stored. Characters are actually converted to integers when they are stored, so you define a character using its numeric value or a character value. Usable character numeric values are from 32 to 127. You'll need to Google the lookup graph to find the numeric value that matches a character.

Let's take a look at both ways to initialize a character.

```
char ch1(97);
char ch2('a');
```

Both of these characters are initialized with the same value. The first ch1 character variable is initialized in its raw numeric format. The second ch2 variable is initialized with the character you want to use. In this example, the character 'a' is used. The character 'a' translates to a numeric value of 97.

Even when you initialize a character with its numeric value, the output will display its associated character value. Let's take a look at some sample code.

```
#include <iostream>

int main()
{
```

```
    char ch(97);
    std::cout << ch;
    return 0;
}
```

In the above code, the output displayed is the character 'a' even though the initialization variable is set to 97. Most programmers don't know the numeric value that matches a character, so they use the character initialization method. However, you might need to know the matching character and number at one point. The best way to work with the mapping is to Google a printout of the information.

With the above method, you would need to create an array of characters to create a string. Unlike C, C++ makes it much easier. Instead of creating arrays, we let the string library do it for us. We add the string library to our include statement.

Let's take a look at the code.

```
#include <string>
#include <iostream>

int main()
{
    std::string myName("John");
    std::cout << "My name is: " << myName;

    return 0;
}
```

The initialization for a string is similar to a character. The one difference is that we set the data type to a string. You'll also notice the string library added at the top of the code. You'll need this library to use strings in this manner.

Notice another difference is that you use the quote character instead of the single tick mark in the character definition. This is standard across most languages. The quote characters indicate a string while the tick mark indicates a character definition.

The string variable is given the name myName and initialized to "John." The string library converts this value to a character array behind the scenes, so you don't need to deal with any of the loops and memory allocation.

Finally, the string is printed to the string using the cout function we saw in chapter 1.

You can also define numeric values as strings. It's not common, but it does happen occasionally. For instance, user input is first sent as a string and then later converted to an integer in your program. Let's take a look at an example.

```
#include <string>
#include <iostream>

int main()
{
    std::string myNumber("45");
    std::cout << "My name is: " << myNumber;

    return 0;
}
```

We didn't change much in this program other than the variable name and value. The value is a number, but it's set in quotes, so the computer sees it as a string.

What happens when you want to get input from a user in the form of a string? C++ has the cin function, which does the opposite of cout. The cin function takes input from the user. The problem with cin is that it only gets a string up until it reaches the first whitespace character such as a space. When it reaches this character, it stops the input. You can use cin for single character input, but we use getline to get full phrases including whitespaces.

Let's take a look at an example.

```
#include <string>
#include <iostream>

int main()
{
    std::cout << "Enter your full name: ";
    std::string fullname;
    std::getline(std::cin, fullname);

    std::cout << "Your name is " << fullname ;
    return 0;
}
```

Now we have a little more complex program compared to our previous Hello World example. This program actually prompts the user for input, takes the user input, and then displays it back to the user.

The first line displays the prompt to the user. The next line defines the variable. The getline statement is the first time we've seen something different. This line stops program execution until the user enters a value and presses Enter on the keyboard. Whatever the user enters, the getline statement retrieves this value. The value is stored in the fullname variable, and then the output is redisplayed on the monitor.

You'll work with string values often in your C++ programs, so they are good to understand early in a programming career.

Boolean Values

Boolean values are the last common variable you'll see in C++ programming. Booleans are the true and false values in C++. Some languages make you use a 1 and 0 to indicate true and false. C++ lets you use the key syntax statement true and false.

When you work with Booleans, you should know that although you see the word "true" in your code, the value is really a bit value 1. The value false is actually a bit value of zero. Booleans are the smallest values, because they only need one bit of storage.

To declare a Boolean in C++, you only need to use the shorthand bool to indicate the data type. Let's look at some sample code.

bool over21 = true;

The statement above initializes the variable over21 and sets it to a Boolean value of true. Once again, this true value is 1.

Boolean values are usually used to control conditional control of the code execution. Let's take a look at an example.

```
#include <iostream>

int main()
{
    bool b = true;
    if (b)
    {
        cout << "B is true";
```

```
    }
    return 0;
}
```

In this example, the Boolean variable b is set to true. The if statement (which we will discuss in chapter 6) evaluates if the b variable is true. If so, the printout is displayed. Since b is always true in this case, the statement "B is true" always displays.

Booleans are a way to evaluate if a statement is true or false, so you can redirect the execution to the appropriate lines of code. They are used often in loops and conditional statements.

Constants

We've covered some basic variable types, but we still have one more to cover. Constants are what they sound like – they are constant values that never change. Constants are beneficial when you want to define a friendly variable name for a value. It's generally not recommended to use static values throughout your code including strings and numbers. To compensate, the programmer should use constants.

Let's take a look at some sample code.

const float MYFACTOR { 1.1 };

The const keyword is what tells the compiler that you want to create a constant. You still need to give your constant a data type, and we decide to give this the floating point decimal float data type.

The interesting part of this statement is that we've given our variable a name with all capital letters. C++ is a case sensitive language, so the variables myfactor, MYFACTOR, myFactor are all different variables in C++. You would never create three variables with the same name but different case, but you should be aware that they are different variables as you type your code. We use all capital letters in this statement because the variable is a constant. It's not required by the compiler, but it's required by coding standards. Most coding standards that you will have to follow during your career call for constants to be set as all capital letters.

After we name our variable, we then set its value in brackets. Remember that a constant value doesn't change, so this is the value the constant has regardless of where it is located in your code. As a matter of fact, if you attempt to change the value, the compiler will give you an error. For instance, the following code gives you a compiler error.

```
const float MYFACTOR { 1.1 };
MYFACTOR = 10.0;
```

The above code throws an error. When you create a constant, always determine if you need a static variable or a dynamic one. Most programs have a few constants, but you should normally create a dynamic variable. For instance, if you have a website URL for an API, you would set it as a constant. If you need to retrieve a URL depending on user input, you would create a dynamic variable.

We covered several concepts in this chapter. Variables and data types are the very foundation of a C++ program, so although they are easier concepts, they are just as important to understand as more complex concepts.

Lab Questions

1. When you want to define a decimal value in C++, what is the data type used to declare the variable?

a. decimal
b. integer
c. float
d. point

Explanation: The float variable type lets you allocate memory for a decimal value and store decimal numbers in your variable.

2. When you define a Boolean value of true, what is the actual value stored in memory?

a. 0
b. 1
c. true
d. yes

Explanation: Boolean values are converted to either 1 or 0. A true value equals 1 and a false value equals 0.

3. What function should you use to obtain string input from a user in C++?

a. getline
b. get
c. cin
d. input

Explanation: The getline function should be used to obtain input from users. The cin function works as well, but it stops when it reaches a whitespace character. To ensure you get all input from the user, always use the getline function.

4. What does the string library do with string input in C++?

a. store it in one long area of memory
b. turn each character into separate characters
c. turn the string into a character array
d. escape each character before storing it

Explanation: String values are actually character arrays in C and C++. C++ has a string library that does the character array manipulations for you.

Chapter 4: Operators

Objective: This chapter covers the arithmetic and comparison operators that are seen in almost any C++ program.

We had a brief overview of operators, but this chapter focuses on operators in detail. Even the smallest C++ program uses an operator. You need to understand how they work, their precedence to properly calculate values, and any comparisons and their outcomes. We'll cover the most common operators with a few uncommon ones as well.

Basic Arithmetic

In just about any C++ program, you'll need to perform some kind of arithmetic. Even when your program requires no arithmetic at all, you'll need to use arithmetic to loop through statements, find indexes in arrays, and keep track of records. Arithmetic is important in any program along with a lot of knowledge.

Let's take a look at a simple program.

```
int num1 = 5;
int num2 = 6;
int num3 = num1 * num2;
```

We've been using addition and subtraction for most of our samples, so this time we decided to add some multiplication. In the above code, we create two variables named num1 and num2 and assign them a value.

We then create a third variable named num3 and assign the product of num1 and num2 to num3. This is a very basic example of operators and how they work with variables. You can, of course, use static numbers that create a value to hold in a variable. The following code would have the same results as the above.

```
int num3 = 5 * 6;
```

The above code only performed one calculation, but as with any calculation, you must know the order of precedence for operations. C++ follows the same precedence as any regular math calculation. You also have precedence of other operators. Since there are numerous operators, most C++ developers have to look up the order of precedence before defining long algorithms and calculations. You can Google these precedence operators and keep a list of them for future use.

Another great reason to learn C++ is that the laws of precedence are followed by other languages. If you learn them in C++, you should know them for any other languages you decide to learn.

Let's take a look at a calculation with different operators.

```
int num1 = 8 * 3 + 1 + 1;
```

If you remember your math classes, you should know the way this problem should play out. Multiplication always takes precedence over addition and subtraction, so the 8 and 3 are the first calculations, and then the 1 values are added. The result of the calculation is 26.

Let's take a look another sample.

int num1 = 8 * 3 + 1 + 1 * 7 + 1;

Now that you know the order of precedence, you can correctly identify the result of the calculation. The result of the first two numbers – 8 and 3 – is first multiplied. Then, the result of the 1 and 7 multiplication is calculated. After these two values are calculated, then the addition is done. The result of the above calculation is 33.

You can also perform shortcut operations on the addition and subtraction activity. C++ has an increment and decrement operator that acts as a shortcut to these operations. Let's take a look at an example.

int num1 = 1;
int num2 = num1++;

The two variables initialized both contain integer values. The first value is set as 1. The num2 variable is initialized and set as the incremented value of num1. The incremented number is the same as saying "add 1 to the variable value." In this case, the value is initialized as 1, so the incremented value is set to 2 and then assigned to num2.

You can also decrement numbers in the same way except using the minus operator. Let's take a look at an example.

int num1 = 1;
int num2 = num1--;

The above code performs the same calculation process except it decrements the value by 1. In other words, subtract 1 from the variable num1 and then save the result in the num2 variable. The result of the calculation is that num2 contains the value 0.

Another useful but different operator is the modulus operation. When you work with even numbers, you'll work with modulus. The modulus operator returns the remainder of a division operation. For instance, if you divide 5 by 2, the modulus operator returns 1. It's a handy tool for looping through numbers and figuring out if the number is even or odd. If the number has no remainder after dividing by 2, then it's an even number. If it has a remainder after dividing by two, then you know it's an odd number.

Let's take a look at an example.

```
int num1 = 1;
int num2 = 3;
float num3 = num1 % 2;
float num4 = num2 % 2;
```

We added several lines to this code. The first two variables are set to hold a static value, which is one and three. The third variable named num3 is used to identify if num1 is an even number. Since 1 divided by 2 equals .5, we know that it's not an even number. Notice that we accounted for fractions by defining this variable as a floating point value.

The next statement evaluates the number 3. We know that the number three is not an even number either, so the modulus statement returns 1. If we used an even number the return value would be 0, which would then signal to our program that we've found an even number.

For more advanced calculations, you might need to call a function. For instance, there is no character for using exponents. C++ provides you with a function called pow to handle exponents. Let's take a look at an example.

```
pow(base, exp);
```

This is the pow template. The base is the number base parameter, and the exp parameter is what you want to raise the base to – in other words it stands for the exponent.

Let's look at a real example.

```
int basenum = 4;
int result = pow(basenum, 2);
```

In this example, we first create a variable named basenum. This variable contains the value 4. We then use the pow function to calculate the basenum variable to the power of 2. The result of the calculation is 16. This makes exponents much easier to use than in other languages that don't support exponents.

Before you create any complex functions, do a lookup on the C++ library to ensure that the compiler doesn't already have a solution for you. Most basic math calculations have a corresponding library for you to use.

Comparison Operators

We just went over most of the basic math operators available in C++. Comparison operators are also important to know, and they are a large portion of most programs. In most programs, you'll need to work with comparison operators. These operators are also referred to as relational operators.

There are several comparison operators. Here are a list of them.

Greater than -- >
Less than -- <
Greater than or equals -- >=
Less than or equals -- <=

Equality -- ==
Inequality -- !=

We'll cover these operators in detail to help you understand how to work with them.

You can look at these operators in the same way you would look at them if you were solving a math problem. Let's first take a look at the greater than and less than statements.

```
int num1 = 1;
int num2 = 2;
if (num1 > num2)
{
        cout << "Greater than";
}
if (num1 < num2)
{
        cout << "Less than";
}
```

We haven't worked with conditions yet, but just know that the if statement is used closely with comparison operators. The first if statement compares the num1 and num2 variables. The first condition checks if num1 is greater than num2. Since the result is false, the if statements are skipped and execution moves on to the next if statement.

The next if statement compares if num1 is less than num2. This statement is different than the first, and the result is true. Since the result is true, the next step of execution is set at the statement within the if statement. In this example, the phrase "Less than" is displayed to the user.

Note that if the numbers are equal, neither of these if statements are executed.

This is a problem when you need to know if a number is greater than or less than or equal to a value. Let's use the same example we have above but change the values of the num1 and num2 variables.

```
int num1 = 1;
int num2 = 1;
if (num1 >= num2)
{
        cout << "Greater than";
}
if (num1 <= num2)
{
        cout << "Less than";
}
```

Now our variables are both equal to 1. They are neither greater than nor less than each other, but we've changed our if statement code. Since the logic is changed, the code execution greatly changed. The first if statement evaluates to true, and the phrase "Greater than" displays to the user.

In the next if statement, true is also evaluated again. Since this if statement evaluates to true as well, the value "Less than" is displayed to the user.

So far, it seems simple enough! But how do we avoid executing an if statement when we only want to execute statements when the values are equal but not greater than, less than or equal. The C++ language includes an equal operator. We mentioned it briefly, because it's similar to the equal assignment operator. Let's take a look at an example using the same code we used previously.

```
int num1 = 1;
int num2 = 1;
```

```
if (num1 == num2)
{
        cout << "Greater than";
}
if (num1 <= num2)
{
        cout << "Less than";
}
```

We set our variables at the same values again. Both of our variables are set to 1. We kept both of the if statements. The first if statement evaluates if the values are equal. Note that the two equal signs are a comparison operator but one equal sign is an assignment operator. If you accidentally use the single equal sign in an if statement, your compiler will return an error.

The next statement is set to less than or equal to. Since both of these variables evaluate to true, both the "Greater than" and "Less than" phrases are printed to the screen.

We've covered greater than, less than, equal to and a combination. However, we still have one more comparison operator to cover. What if we need to know if a pair of variables is not equal? None of these comparison operators will work for what we need. The C++ language includes a not equal to comparison operator, so you can perform this action.

Let's use the above samples for our new comparison operator.

```
int num1 = 1;
int num2 = 1;
if (num1 == num2)
{
        cout << "Greater than";
}
```

```
if (num1 != num2)
{
        cout << "Less than";
}
```

We've used the same num1 and num2 variables. We also set them to the same value. They are both assigned a value of 1. Now, we want to know if the variables are equal, and then we want to know if the variables are not equal.

The first if statement uses the equality comparison operator again. The result is true so the phrase "Greater than" is displayed to the user. The change in our sample was in the second if statement. This statement evaluates if the two variables are not equal. In this example, the two variables are indeed equal, so the result is false. Whenever an if comparison evaluates to false, the compiler skips the if statements code and moves on to the next line of code. Since we have no other lines of code to execute, the program terminates.

You can use compound comparisons in your if statements. We will get into conditions in chapter 6, so we don't want to get too detailed with if statements in this chapter. This chapter's purpose is to explain operators. Just know that you can compound conditional evaluations. We'll take a look at compound comparisons in chapter 6.

Comparison operators and arithmetic operators are an important part of any C++ program. You'll run into them often either in your own code or maintenance of another program. A simple mistake in conditional statements can lead to severe bugs, so it's important to understand how they work before you code any program. It takes some practice to understand code execution with these operators, so use this lesson to practice with your own programs and code.

Lab Questions

1. If you have a calculation that contains an addition operator and a multiplication operator, which one takes precedence?

a. the multiplication operator
b. the addition operator
c. neither, they are equal
d. they negate each other

Explanation: multiplication takes precedence over addition statements, so always calculate the multiplication before you calculate addition operations.

2. You have the following calculation in your C++ code:

int result = 6+ 1 + 5 * 4;

What is the value contained in the result variable?

a. 26
b. 25
c. 27
d. 40

Explanation: The 5 and 4 multipliers are first evaluated, and then the addition calculations are performed.

3. What is the correct comparison operator to use when you want to evaluate if two variables are not equal?

a. <=
b. ==
c. >=
d. !=

Explanation: The != operator evaluates if two values are not equal. If this comparison operator is used in an if statement and the result is true, the if statements are executed.

4. What C++ function do you use to perform exponential functions?

a. exp
b. base
c. pow
d. multiply

Explanation: The pow function takes a base and exponent value and performs exponent multiplication calculations.

Chapter 5: Advanced Data Types

<u>Objective:</u> This chapter covers more advanced data types. We've covered basics, but this chapter gives you an overview of scopes, enumerations, and structures.

We covered a few variable types in previous chapters, but C++ provides developers with several other more complex data types to allow for easier programming. You can even make your own data types. When you create classes, these classes become your custom data types. The standard data type is called a primitive. Integers, floating point decimals, and characters are primitive data types. We're going to explore more complex data types and understand how they relate to C++.

Enumerators

Enumerators are an example of creating your own data type. The enum data type creates a list of values that contain their own numeric constant. The constant is called an enumerator. You use these data types when you have a list of constant values that you need to represent with a symbolic variable. Let's take a look at some sample code to understand enumerators better.

```
enum Color
{
  BLUE,
  BLACK,
  RED
};
```

You can say that the Color data type has been enumerated. Notice that the enumeration has the opening and closing brackets just like the if statements and functions we've seen in previous chapters.

These data types are used in the same way you create a class or function. If you recall from a previous chapter, we set up a function by first defining its data type, then defining a name for the function, and then all code within the brackets are considered a part of the function.

The same is true with an enumerated data type. In this example, we set the enum data type and define the name. In this example, we've decided that we need a list of colors. Note that enumerated values should not by dynamic. For instance, you wouldn't have a set of Color values and then change the list to birds. You wouldn't decide that you need to dynamically add a new color to the enumerator. You always know the list of values that you need, because enumerators act as constants for your data types.

With this enumerator, we have a list of colors. We only want three colors. Each color is separated by a comma except for the last color. If you accidentally add a comma at the end of the last color, the compiler will return an error.

You probably notice that we gave the color names set in all capital letters. In any coding language, constants are set in all capital letters. It's not required by the compiler, but it is a part of coding standards. We covered constants and their naming schemes in chapter 3.

Our Color data type is not exactly the same as a standard constant, but the enumerated values within the brackets are static.

You might ask yourself what these constants represent. What are their values? The C++ language assigns these constants a value. They are assigned a value in the order they appear. Let's take a look at the Color enumerated value with some comments.

```
enum Color
{
  BLUE, // value of 0
  BLACK, // value of 1
  RED // value 2
};
```

We've added some comments to the enumerated data type. Remember that comments are ignored by the compiler, so you can comment your code as much as you want.

Enumerated values are always given a value starting at 0. Each variable is given its own incremented value. This means that blue has a value of 0, the next variable black gets the value of 1, and then the next variable gets the value of 2. When you call these variables in your code, these are the values they have during execution.

Another important aspect about these data types is that once you give an enumerator a list of variable names, you cannot use those names in any other sections of the code. These variable names are globally defined, which means they are accessible in any section of your code. Let's look at an example.

```
enum Color
{
  BLUE, // value of 0
  BLACK, // value of 1
  RED // value 2
```

```
};

enum MoreColors
{
  BLUE, // value of 0
  GREEN, // value of 1
  ORANGE // value 2
};
```

The above code would throw a compiler error, because you've already used the BLUE variable name in the original Color enumeration.

Now that you have your Color data type defined, you can use it in your code. Let's take a look at how you would define a variable and obtain its value.

```
enum Color
{
  BLUE, // value of 0
  BLACK, // value of 1
  RED // value 2
};
Color paint = BLUE;
std::cout << paint;
```

In the example code, we have our data type definition, and then we decide to use it in some code. Because Color is now a data type, we use it to define a variable. We decide to create the variable paint with the data type of Color. We then give the variable a constant value from our list of colors. Because the BLUE constant value is 0, the next statement prints out the value of 0 to the user.

Because enumerated variables have a list of constants with integer values, you can also use them to initialize an integer variable. For instance, the following code is also valid.

int paintcolor = BLUE;

The compiler implicitly converts the BLUE constant to an integer and assigns it to the paintcolor variable. The compiler won't be able to convert an integer value to the enumerated data type. For instance, the following code gives you an error.

Color paint = 0;

The above code gives you an error, because the compiler is not able to convert an integer to the color data type. Just remember that enumerated values are integers and can be stored in integer variables, but you can't go in the opposite direction by assigning the enumeration with an integer value.

Structures

Structures are similar but much different code architecture. Structures give you a way to represent objects without defining cumbersome variables.

For instance, let's say you have a program that gets a list of employee information. Each employee has a first and last name that you need to retrieve. You then need to get a birth date's year, month and day. You could create these variables separately, or you could use a structure to better define and represent your information.

Let's say you need to log information for two employees. Your variables would look like the following.

std::string firstname1;

```cpp
std::string firstname2;
std::string lastname1;
std::string lastname2;
std::string birthyear1;
std::string birthyear2;
```

As you can see, this type of variable definition is completely inefficient. A structure lets you create a class or an object for the employee, and then you can assign the class properties with values that represent each employee.

Let's take a look at the code needed to create an employee structure.

```cpp
struct Employee
{
    int id;
    std::string firstname;
    std::string lastname;
    int birthyear;
};
```

You'll notice that structures are defined in a similar was as enumerations. However, structures have more complexities. Instead of giving an automatic integer value to each structure property, you can define your own value for each property. Also, structure property values can be dynamic, so you aren't stuck with only constants as an option. The above code is much more efficient than creating variables for both of your employees.

Now that we have the structure declared, we can use it in our code. Let's take a look at how you can use your structure.

```cpp
struct Employee
{
```

```
        int id;
        std::string firstname;
        std::string lastname;
        int birthyear;
};
Employee john;
Employee jane;
```

The above code defines our Employee structure, and then it uses the structure to define two variables named john and jane. Like enumerations, structures are also their own data types. The Employee data type is used to create the two jane and john variables.

With our structures defined, now let's look at how we can assign values to them. The following code assigns values to both jane and john.

```
struct Employee
{
        int id;
        std::string firstname;
        std::string lastname;
        int birthyear;
};
Employee john;
john.firstname = "John";
john.lastname = "Smith";
john.birthyear = 2000;
Employee jane;
jane.firstname = "John";
jane.lastname = "Smith";
jane.birthyear = 2000;
```

This is much more organized and easier to read than the previous variables we used. We still define two employees, but it's easier to read and understand. If you call the Employee variable john, you know where you stored the first name.

Structures make it much easier to remember your variables and what data they store. It also makes it easier to read and understand your code when a secondary programmer must maintain it. You can also use the cout function to display the information when you populate the structure. Let's complete the structure program with an example of using output to display the employee's first name.

```cpp
struct Employee
{
    int id;
    std::string firstname;
    std::string lastname;
    int birthyear;
};
Employee john;
john.firstname = "John";
john.lastname = "Smith";
john.birthyear = 2000;
Employee jane;
jane.firstname = "John";
jane.lastname = "Smith";
jane.birthyear = 2000;
cout << jane.firstname;
```

In this example, we just printed Jane's first name, which of course is "Jane." If you used the cumbersome variable names, you would need to scroll up your code and recall which variable contained what employee information.

This code lets you simply call jane's data, and you know that you're getting jane's information.

Enumerators and structures are much more complex data types, but they are extremely useful when you start to build robust applications. You'll need to keep your code organized and easy to read. If you don't, it's very difficult to manage. You might have other programmers working with your code, and they won't be able to easily understand your intentions. When code is more difficult to read, there is a much higher chance that any additions will cause bugs in the future.

You can use structures and enumerators to create new data types, which can then be loaded into other areas of your code. These data types are commonly used in includes and class designs in larger applications.

Lab Questions

1. What value is given to the first constant in an enumerated variable?

a. 0
b. 1
c. 2
d. null

Explanation: the first variable value in an enumerated variable data type is always 0.

2. When you see a variable in all capital letters, what can you assume about the variable?

a. that it's a global variable
b. that it's a constant
c. that it's a local variable

d. that it contains an integer

Explanation: Coding standards ask that developers create constant variables in all capital letters. While it's not a guarantee, it's standard to assume that a variable is a constant if it's in all capital letters in your code.

3. Suppose you have a structure named Employee. You define an Employee variable named john. This structure has a firstname property defined in the structure. Write the code that assigns the firstname property for john with the value of "John."

```
Employee john;
john.firstname = "John";
```

Explanation: Structures create a custom data type. The first line of code defines the john variable using the Employee data type. Once the variable is defined, you can assign values to the structures properties. In this example, the structure has a firstname property that takes string input.

Chapter 6: Loops and Conditional Statements

Objective: Loops and conditional statements control the process flow for code execution. This chapter explains loops and conditional statements in detail.

Loops and conditional statements are grouped into a programming concept called logic control. Both of these statements are logical statements used to evaluate variables and respond with either true or false. When the statement results in a true response, specific statements run. Conversely, if the statement results in a false value, statements are either skipped or the compiler is given an alternative set of instructions. Loops and conditional statements are very common in any C++ program, so it's important for any new developer to understand the processes.

The if Statement

The C++ if statement falls into the conditional statement category. It's the main conditional statement that you'll use when you create your programs. The switch statement is an alternative, but the if conditional statement is much more popular with coding standards. The if statement can evaluate one or more variables, and you can even use compound comparisons in your statements.

We covered if statements very briefly in chapter 4, and now we're going to explain them in better detail.

First, let's take a look at the standard if statement template.

```
if (condition)
{
   //statements that run when condition is true
}
```

If you recall from chapter 4, when the condition within parenthesis returns true, the statements within brackets are executed. What we didn't show you in chapter 4 is that you can set up alternative statements when the result is false. Let's take a look at the if-else statement.

```
if (condition)
{
   //statements that run when condition is true
}
else
{
   //statements that run when the condition is false
}
```

Now, let's take a look at an if statement in action.

```
int num1 = 5;
int num2 = 6;
int result = num1 + num2;
if (result > 4)
{
  cout << "Result is greater than 4.";
}
else
{
  cout << "Result is less than 4.";
}
```

The above if statement is simple. If the result of the addition of num1 and num2 is greater than 4, then the phrase "Result is greater than 4" is displayed. If it's not, the alternative phrase "Result is less than 4" displays. Since the comparison of 4 with the result variable is true, the first statement is displayed. The alternative "else" statement only executes if the condition is evaluated to true.

You might see an issue with this code. What happens if the result is equal to 4? The condition results in a false response, so the else statements are executed. The problem is that the phrase results in "Result is less than 4," which is inaccurate.

We can change our if statement to perform compound comparisons. C++ doesn't limit you to just one comparison like we've seen in previous examples. You can perform multiple comparisons and use logic operations to determine the output. Let's take a look at an example.

```cpp
int num1 = 5;
int num2 = 6;
int result = num1 + num2;
if (result > 4 )
{
  cout << "Result is greater than 4.";
}
else if (result == 4)
{
  cout << "Result is equal to 4.";
}
else
{
  cout << "Result is less than 4.";
}
```

Now our if statement accounts for equality. If result is equal to four, control is sent to the else-if section of the if structure. You can continue to stack these if and if-else statements together to account for each logical possibility in your code.

If statements can get complex and difficult to read. If you have too many stacked if and if-else statements, coding standards ask that you create a function. We'll get into functions in chapter 8, but know that functions are used when there are too many logical possibilities. Functions are more efficient, and they are easier to read and understand. Too many if statements can lead to logic bugs.

The switch Statement

The switch statement is an alternative to the if statement. The switch statement does similar control flow except it does not do comparisons like the if statement. As we mentioned in the previous section, you can have several stacked if-else statements. However, when you get too many in a row, it becomes more difficult to read and debug. The alternative (besides building a function) is to use the switch statement, which is cleaner and easier to read.

Let's assume we have a list of colors using a structure we created in the previous chapter. If you recall, we created a structure named color. Here is the code again.

```
enum Color
{
  BLUE,
  BLACK,
  RED
};
```

Suppose we have a variable we need to evaluate. You could write 3 or 4 if-else statements, or you could use the switch statement. Because switch statements are easier to read, they are preferred when you need several comparisons.

Let's first take a look at what the code would look like if we used an if statement.

```
Color color = BLUE;
if (color == BLUE)
{
   cout << "Color is blue.";
}
else if (color == BLACK)
{
   cout << "Color is black.";
}
else if (color == RED)
{
   cout << "Color is red.";
}
else
{
   cout << "Don't know the color.";
}
```

The above code works, but it's much more difficult to read than the following switch statement.

```
Color color = BLUE;
switch (color)
   {
      case BLUE:
         std::cout << "Blue";
         break;
      case BLACK:
```

```cpp
            std::cout << "Black";
            break;
        case RED:
            std::cout << "Red";
            break;
        default:
            std::cout << "Unknown";
            break;
    }
```

As you can see, this code is much cleaner and accomplishes the same result as the previous if statements. The default statement is similar to the else statement. If no color is found, the default statement runs and displays "Unknown."

The switch statement has a slightly different way of executing than the if statement. The if statement does a comparison, but the switch statement only performs an equality comparison. The switch statement determines the variable you want to compare. In this example, we want to review the color variable.

Once the variable for comparison is determine, the execution flow falls to the first case statement. The first case statement determines if the color variable equals blue. In this example, the result is true. If it was not true, the next case statement executes. Each case statement executes in the order in which it's coded. If no color is found, only then will the default statements execute.

When a case statement evaluates to true, the statements within the case statement executes. In this example, we simply display the color that we found. The break statements are important in the execution flow. The break statement tells the switch command to stop executing.

If you don't add a break statement to each case, the next case statement executes. The break statement is used to stop the comparison or the execution will continue until it meets with the default statement. The default statement would also run, and then you'd get a color and an unknown response from the program. This, of course, would be a bug in your code.

The while and do while Loops

The while loop is much more common than the do while loop, but it's important to know both structures. These two loops control execution flow by evaluating a condition and looping until that condition is met. For instance, suppose you want to print values from 0 to 3. Instead of writing three output statements, you can write one loop statement and dynamically display the values until all four values are displayed.

Let's see an example of the code.

```
int count = 0;
while(count < 4)
{
    cout << count << "\n";
    count++;
}
```

In the above code, we first initiate our variable that contains the numeric values. Execution then falls to the while loop. The while loop evaluates if the count variable is less than 4. As long as this condition returns true, the while loop continues to run. Since we initialize the count variable to 0, the first run of the while loop evaluates to true.

Next, we have the statements within the while loop brackets. Any code within these brackets execute with each loop. We only have two statements within the while loop brackets.

The while loop's first statement is to print the value. In this example, the first value is 0.

The next statement is imperative to avoid a bug called an infinite loop. An infinite loop occurs when the while loop's condition always returns true, and there is no condition that stops it from looping. Infinite loops fill a computer's memory, and it crashes the program. You'll run into infinite loops as you code and debug your programs. If we removed the count increment statement, we would create an infinite loop.

The count variable starts at 0 and the loop continues to execute until count reaches the number 4. Once the value is 4, the while loop executes and any statements under it continue to execute.

The alternative to a while loop is a do while loop. A do while loop works the same way, except the statements within the loop always execute once. With a while loop, if we set the count variable to 5, the loop would never execute. But if we used a do while loop, even setting the count variable to 5 wouldn't stop the statements from running at least once. Let's take a look at the same logic but with a do while loop.

```
int count = 4;
do
{
  cout << count << "\n";
  count++;
}
while(count < 4);
```

We changed the initialization value to 4 and changed the while loop to a do while loop.

You'll notice that the while condition evaluates to false, but the statements are set prior to the condition. In this example, the printout shows 4 to the user and then increments the count variable by one. Since the count variable would then be 5, the while execution terminates and the next statements are shown.

These small logic differences can make huge changes to your program. Part of writing great software is knowing how to design it properly. You'll need to make decisions on what type of loop is the most efficient for you code without causing any logic errors.

The for Loop

The for loop is the most common loop that you'll run into when you code. For loops have an incrementing value in the condition statement, so it's much less likely that you'll cause an infinite loop when you use them. With the while loop, you have to ensure that you use some kind of breakout method, but with the for loop the breakout procedure is built in.

Let's take a look at the for loop template.

```
for (initialization statement ; condition ; increment expression)
{
// for loop statements go here
}
```

The initialization statement is the variable you want to use in the condition. Normally, this value is 0. The next part of the loop is the condition that you want to evaluate. If the condition evaluates to true, the loop continues. If it evaluates to false, the for loop stops execution. The final section of the for loop is the increment expression.

This increment is placed on the initialization variable in the first section. Let's take a look at some example code. We'll use the same logic we used for the while statement. We want to create a loop that prints out the numbers 0 to 3.

```
for (int count=0; count < 4; count++)
{
   cout << count << " ";
}
```

You'll notice that we're using the same variables. The count variable is initialized to 0. We want to continue to loop as long as count is less than 4. Each time the for loop iterates, the count variable is incremented by one. Note that the count variable is not incremented on the first loop. The for loop initializes the variable, evaluates if the condition is true, and then loops. Only on the second loop is the count variable incremented.

The advantage of this loop is that you don't need to remember the increment statement. If you didn't include the increment statement, the compiler gives you an error.

These loops and conditional statements are engrained in any program. You'll need a firm grasp of them to properly debug code. They are common in code, but they are also likely culprits for causing bugs. Just one small logic error in your code can cause huge bugs in your program. For this reason, it's important to design your code well and use the most efficient structure that makes the code easy to read if you ever need to change it.

Lab Questions

1. What type of loop is created when you define a while loop that never stops executing?

a. do while
b. for while
c. infinite loop
d. double loop

Explanation: an infinite loop eats up computer memory and eventually crashes your program.

2. What statement must you include in a switch statement to ensure that execution stops after a case matches?

a. goto
b. break
c. default
d. switch

Explanation: the break statement stops execution within the switch statement, so every case evaluation doesn't run.

3. What loop always executes its statements at least once?

a. do while
b. while
c. for
d. switch

Explanation: the do while loop executes its statements first, and then it evaluates the condition. This means that statements always run at least once.

4. What type of loop has a smaller chance of creating an infinite loop since the increment expression is embedded in the loop structure?

a. do while
b. while

c. for
d. switch

Explanation: the for loop is the preferred loop for logical execution flow, because it contains the increment expression and the condition embedded in its structure.

Chapter 7: Arrays and Pointers

Objective: This chapter covers arrays and their indexes as well as the pointers that link values and variables to a memory location.

Arrays and pointers are slightly more advanced concepts. Arrays are a part of every program, because you can contain several values in only 1 variable. You can contain 1 or 1000 values in one variable. Pointers are one of the most difficult for students to understand, because you point to specific areas of memory and not an actual value. We'll cover both of these concepts in this chapter, so you can get a full understanding of them.

Building Arrays

There are times when you need to calculate or evaluate several records. We used an example of an employee record using structures where we wanted to fill two records with the same type of data. But what if you had 100 employee records that you needed to work with? You could use an array, which would hold each value in a separate container. These containers are called indexes.

An index is a location within the array. When you code your programs, you'll increment and iterate through these indexes. An important part of indexes is understanding where they start. Indexes always start at 0.

First, let's look at the code to initialize an array.

```
int numbers[2];
```

That's all it takes to initialize an array, but there are concepts you should know. The int data type tells the compiler that you want to contain integer values in your array. The data type set on an array defines the type of data you can store in the variable. In this example, we want to store integer values.

The next part of the statement is the array name. We've given the name "numbers" to the array. The number 2 in brackets defines the number of values you can store in the array. In this example, we set the number of possible values to 2. An important issue to note is that you don't store numbers 1 to 2. The 2 in the brackets is the amount of values you can store, but array indexes start with 0. This means that the indexes for the array are 0 and 1. Remember that the index containers start with 0, and the last index container is the number in brackets minus 1. In this instance, it's 2-1 or 1.

After you create the array, you can now populate it with values. You use the index numbers to assign values to the array. Let's take a look at some code.

```
int numbers[2];
numbers[0] = 1;
numbers[1] = 3;
```

In the above code, we've filled both indexes with a value. You don't have to fill the array with values immediately after you create the array. Most programs use a for loop to populate an array with its values. For instance, suppose you want to populate the numbers array using a for loop and the count variable we worked with in the last chapter.

If you wanted to populate the array using a loop, here is an example of how you could do it.

```
int numbers[2];
for (int count = 0; count < 2; count++)
{
    numbers [count] = count;
}
```

In the above code, we first define the array. We again set the array to contain 2 values. We then use the count variable that we worked with in the previous chapter. We initialize it to 0, and start the loop. Notice that we used count in the array value assignment. In the first iteration, count is equal to 0. This means that the first iteration populates the array container at index 0. Then, count is incremented by 1, and the index container of 1 is populated next this is an important concept when you start working with large sets of data. We could change these values to 100 without changing our code and creating massive lines code. This is the advantage of an array working with a for loop.

Arrays and for loops are also used to display information. Just like the above loop where we assigned values, we can also loop through an array just to display the information. Let's take a look at an example.

```
int numbers[2];
numbers[0] = 1;
numbers[1] = 3;
for (int count = 0; count < 2; count++)
{
    cout << numbers [count] ;
}
```

In this example, we assigned values to our array. We used the same for loop for assigning values to our array, but this time we just display the information.

Notice that we use the count variable to retrieve information from the numbers array. Even though count is equal to 1 in the second iteration, the display value shown is 3, because 3 is contained in the index container 1.

Arrays aren't limited to containing primitive values. We showed you how to work with simple integers, but you can also use arrays to contain entire structures. In the structure chapter, we discussed creating structures to represent data when you have several variables that you need to create. With structures, you can organize your data more efficiently. We used an example of an Employee structure.

Suppose you needed to store 100 employee structures. An array can be used to store the 100 Employee structure records. Let's take another look at our Employee structure.

```
struct Employee
{
    int id;
    std::string firstname;
    std::string lastname;
    int birthyear;
};
```

Now we want to store several Employee records in an array. If you recall, structures create your own data type. This means that we can define an array variable using the Employee data type. Take a look at the following code.

```
struct Employee
{
    int id;
    std::string firstname;
    std::string lastname;
    int birthyear;
```

```
};
Employee employees[2];
```

In the code above, we have the structure defined, and then we create an array with the data type Employee. The array's name is employees, and we tell the compiler to allocate memory for two Employee structures.

Now let's populate a structure and assign it to the first index container.

```
struct Employee
{
    int id;
    std::string firstname;
    std::string lastname;
    int birthyear;
};
Employee employees[2];
Employee emp1;
emp1.id = 1;
emp1.firstname = "John";
emp1.lastname = "Smith";
emp1.birthyear = 2000;
employees[0] = emp1;
```

As you can see, you populate the structure just like you did in the previous chapters. You then assign the structure to the array. You might wonder what you can do to obtain values from the structure within the array. You could retrieve the entire structure, but you can also retrieve values individually using the array index and the property you want to retrieve. Let's take a look at an example.

```
struct Employee
{
```

```
    int id;
    std::string firstname;
    std::string lastname;
    int birthyear;
};
Employee employees[2];
Employee emp1;
emp1.id = 1;
emp1.firstname = "John";
emp1.lastname = "Smith";
emp1.birthyear = 2000;
employees[0] = emp1;
cout << employees[0].firstname;
```

We added one more line of code to our program. We display the firstname property located in the structure at index 0. This is a basic way to retrieve information, but you can use this method to loop through dozens of employee records and display them to your users. Arrays are the classic way to handle execution when you need to support several records and variable values in one procedure.

Pointers

Pointers are a much more difficult concept. Pointers are variables that point to a specific address space. If you recall from chapter 2, we discussed how memory is reserved for your program and its variables. The compiler requests memory space from the operating system when it defines a variable in your code. The operating system allocates memory and allows the program to store data in each memory address space.

A pointer points to the address space allocated for your variable. You can then print the address space value or the value contained within the address space.

Let's take a look at an example.

```
int mynumber = 5;
int *ptr = &mynumber;
```

Even though this is only two lines of code, there is a lot to understand in these statements. The first statement is the variable assignment we've seen already. The second line of code defines a pointer.

You know a pointer is defined from the asterisk in front of the variable name. We still use the int variable data type, which tells the compiler that the value stored in memory is an integer. Pointer data types must match the values they point to.

When you define a pointer value, you don't assign the typical value you would with a normal variable. Since pointers contain memory address spaces, you must point to a variable's address space. When you place an ampersand (&) in front of a variable, you tell the compiler that you want to retrieve the memory address. In the above code, we assign the memory address space for mynumber to the *ptr pointer variable.

Here is a visual representation to help you understand.

```
0012FFF7C          <--- This is the value of the pointer
------------------
5                  <----- This is the value of the mynumber
```

The 0012FFF7C value is the memory address. This memory address contains the value of 5. As long as you have the address value for the pointer, you can always obtain the value of the variable.

Let's print out some values to view the results of our code.

```
int mynumber = 5;
int *ptr = &mynumber;
cout << mynumber; //prints 5
cout <<*ptr; //prints 5
cout << ptr; //prints 0012FFF7C
cout << &mynumber; //prints 0012FFF7C
```

As you can see from the comments, each pointer and variable value points to either the value of the mynumber variable or the address space. You don't normally use the address space in output, but you will use the pointer and memory address information as you calculate low level procedures.

One issue to note with pointers is that they must be initialized to a valid variable. If you don't initialize the pointer to a variable's memory address, you can possibly crash your program. The reason for this is from the way operating systems handle programs and memory management. When you run your program, the operating system sets aside memory space specific for your program. Programs are sandboxed, which means they are cut off from accessing memory addresses for other programs. This is a security measure to protect data from leaking between programs. It also protects other programs from crashing if yours crashes. Sandboxing is a newer operating system technology, but it's standard in software design.

Let's take a look at some example code. You can run this code in your own programming environment, but it will likely crash. It won't harm the computer, but just know that it will likely crash.

```
#include <iostream>
```

```
int main()
{
    int *ptr;
    std::cout << *ptr;
    return 0;
}
```

In the above program, you'll notice that we don't assign the pointer to any variable. The pointer is pointing to what is referred to as garbage memory. This memory contains no value, so there is nothing to display. When you point to garbage memory values, the program can crash.

You can also use pointers to get the size of a variable's value. This is useful to understand the amount of space used by stored values.

Let's take a look at the code to determine the size of the mynumber variable we created earlier.

```
int mynumber = 5;
int *ptr = &mynumber;
cout << mynumber; //prints 5
cout <<*ptr; //prints 5
cout << ptr; //prints 0012FFF7C
cout << &mynumber; //prints 0012FFF7C
cout << sizeof(ptr);
```

We added one line of code to our previous program. We still print the address memory locations and values for the variable, but now we include the sizeof function. The sizeof function tells you how much memory is used for a variable. This variable is easy to evaluate, because integers take 4 bytes of memory.

However, if you have a large structure, you won't know the amount of space allocated until you use the sizeof function.

Arrays and pointers have several uses, and we just skimmed the details. Since we're just starting out, getting too detailed with pointers and arrays can get confusing. The best way to better understand pointers and arrays is to write small programs and practice with each concept. You might even want to try the program that crashes just to see the output and the compiler's response when it tries to reference garbage memory.

Arrays are more common than pointers, but pointers are used in complex, low-level programs such as gaming engines and embedded system development.

Lab Questions

1. You want to create an array variable named mynumber that can contain two values. Write the code that defines this variable in C++.

int mynumber[2];

Explanation: The number set within the brackets tells the compiler how many values the array can contain. This array can contain 2 integer values.

2. You want to create a pointer named ptr. You want to assign the mynumber array to the pointer. Write the code that initializes the pointer variable and assigns the variable.

int *ptr = &mynumber;

Explanation: Pointer variables always use an asterisks prefix. The ampersand character prefixed in the variable name tells the compiler to assign the variable's address space to the pointer variable.

3. What type of loop is usually used to populate an array's list of values?

a. while
b. do while
c. for
d. switch

Explanation: The for loop lets you assign a specific number of iterations using the array's length, so it's commonly used to populate and display array values.

4. What type of memory is used for allocation when a pointer is not initialized to a variable address?

a. null
b. garbage
c. external
d. sandboxed

Explanation: When the pointer isn't initialized to a variable, it points to garbage memory and often crashes a program if it's referenced.

Chapter 8: Functions

Objective: This chapter teaches you how to make functions, which are the subroutines for C++. Functions create subroutines and additional logic for a program's code execution.

Functions are in every C++ program. If you recall from the first chapters, we included the main function to illustrate a full program. This function is the entry point for a C++ program. This function then calls other functions until the program is finished or closed by the user. Your C++ programs will contain dozens of functions to make one program. This chapter will show you how to create a function, pass parameters overload them and we even explain the concept of the stack and heap.

Creating a Function

We had a brief overview of functions, but let's review them again. The best function to review when starting a C++ programming course is the main function since it's a part of every C++ program.

```
#include <iostream>

int main()
{
    cout << "Hello World";
    return 0;
}
```

The above code is one of the simplest programs in C++. The Hello World program is standard for new developers to help them understand programming concepts. Let's dissect this program line by line.

The include statement we've seen before. This statement includes external libraries. In this example, we've imported the iostream library, which is necessary for the cout function.

Next, the function is defined. The int statement tells the compiler that an integer value is returned after the function is finished executing. All main functions in C++ programs return an integer value. This integer is used to identify if any error is thrown during program execution. When a 0 is returned, it tells the compiler that the program ran successfully.

The main function does not take any parameters, but we'll cover functions and parameters in the next section.

All statements within the brackets are the function's execution code. The function will continue executing until it reaches the return statement. Remember that functions with a data type must return a value, so you must return an integer in this main function. If you tried to return a string, the compiler would give you an error.

You can also use the void data type. Let's take a look at a function with a void data type definition.

```cpp
#include <iostream>

void calculate()
{
        int int1  = 5;
        int int2 = 5;
```

```
        cout << int1 + int2;
}
```

Notice in this calculate function, void is used as the data type.
This tells the compiler that no value is returned. As you can
see, there is no return statement in the function. You can still
use the return statement if you want to terminate the function
prematurely. For instance, if a value evaluates to a specific
condition, you can use the return statement.

Let's take a look at a void statement with a return.

```
#include <iostream>

void calculate()
{
        int int1  = 5;
        int int2 = 5;
        if (int1 == 5)
        {
            return;
        }
        cout << int1 + int2;
}
```

Notice in this return statement that no value is indicated.
Because the function is set to void, any return value creates an
error in your code, and the compiler won't compile it. In this
example code, if the int1 variable is 5, the function terminates
prematurely. Since int1 is actually 5, this function displays
nothing to the user. It's not a logical function to use, but it
gives you a good example of how you can terminate a
function and return execution to the calling function.

Using Parameters with a Function Definition

If you recall from chapter 6, we mentioned that it's better to use functions for decision making when you have too many if-else statements. When a function doesn't take any parameters, there isn't much logic to it. These types of functions are used when you don't need any logic and want to just reuse the same code to calculate values. However, a more common way to use functions is to set parameters in the function and force the calling statement to pass parameters that are then used to calculate logic.

The following is the template for a function with parameters.

```
datatype functionname(param1, param2, …)
{
        // statements to execute
}
```

As you can see, the format is similar to the main function we worked with in the last section. The only difference is we added parameters. You can have any number of parameters in your function, but remember that the number of parameters you set must be used by the calling function. If you have too many parameters, it's best to break down your function into several functions or consider redesigning your code for efficiency.

The template helps us learn the way functions are set up, but it doesn't help when we're trying to learn to code real programs. Let's take a look at an actual function with some real logic.

```
#include <iostream>

int calculate (int x, int y)

int calculate(int x, int y)
```

```
{
        int result = x * y;
        return result;
}
```

We removed the main function for simplicity. There are several concepts to consider in these statements.

First, you'll notice that it looks like we defined the function twice, but we didn't. C++ and even C use a concept called prototyping. You're required to add the prototyping statements at the beginning of you C++ programming files. The prototype is just a copy of the function definition without the actual execution statements. It seems useless, but you'll need it for the compiler. Without the prototype, the compiler gives you an error.

The next statements are the actual function. This function is named calculate, and it takes two integers as a parameter. The parameters in this function are named x and y, but the calling statement does not need the same named function parameters. We'll discuss calling statements after we detail the function.

The x and y parameter variables are then used to multiply the two statements and return a result. It's a simple function, but it has a purpose. The function won't execute unless you call the function somewhere in your code. Let's add our main function back and have it call the calculate function.

```
#include <iostream>

int calculate (int x, int y)

int main()
{
    int result = calculate (5, 5);
```

```
    cout << result;
    return 0;
}

int calculate(int x, int y)
{
        int result = x * y;
        return result;
}
```

Now we have a full program with a calling function and a result returned. The main function calls the calculate function with the two integer parameters. We pass two values of 5 to the calculate function. The calculate function multiples the two values and returns 25 to the calling statement. The 25 value is stored as "result" in the calling statement. Now that we have the result, we print out the value to the screen.

The above program is how you use functions, and how most programs are designed. Large applications have hundreds of functions that call each other to create a full functional C++ program.

Variable Scope

When you work with functions, variable scope is an issue. The variable scope defines where you can obtain a variable's value and if the compiler can recognize the variable if you attempt to use it.

There are two types of scope: global and local. Most variables are local, but constants are often made global.

A local variable is only available within the function. Let's return to the program we created in the previous section.

```cpp
#include <iostream>

int calculate (int x, int y)

int main()
{
    int result = calculate (5, 5);
    cout << result;
    return 0;
}

int calculate(int x, int y)
{
        int result = x * y;
        return result;
}                                    .
```

The x and y variables in the calculate function are local
variables. If you attempt to use them from the main function,
the compiler gives you an error. When the function is called,
the x and y variables are automatically created and initialized
with the values you passed from the calling statement. In this
case, the values initialized are both 5. Once the function sends
the result back to the calling statement, those variables are
then automatically destroyed in memory. They are no longer
available, which is why the compiler will give you an error if
you try to obtain those variables from any other parts of your
code.

Global functions aren't used as much, because they are
considered inefficient compared to local variables but you still
need to use them in sections of your code. Global variables are
available anywhere in the program. Let's add a global
constant variable to our C++ calculation program.

#include <iostream>

```
int calculate (int x, int y);
const int MAININT = 4;

int main()
{
   int result = calculate (5, 5);
    cout << result + MAININT;
   return 0;
}

int calculate(int x, int y)
{
        int result = x * y;
        return result;
}
```

Remember that constants are generally created in all caps. The reason is to help programmers quickly identify a constant as they read the code. As you can see, you know that MAININT is a constant as you read the code. It stands out from the other variables in your code.

Also notice that you can use the MAININT variable anywhere in your code. It's globally available and isn't destroyed until the program closes. Because global variables are always available, they take up more memory than a local variable, which is one reason they are not preferred when they aren't needed.

Function Overloading

We created our calculate function, but it only receives integers. What if you want to multiply decimal values? If you tried to send the calculate function a decimal, the compiler gives you an error, and your program crashes. To overcome this issue, you can make two functions with the same name.

The process is called overloading. Overloading uses the same name as another function, but the return type or variables are different. There must be a difference in the functions return type and/or the number of parameters accepted. If you don't have one of these differences, the program doesn't know what function to use when you call it, and the compiler gives you an error.

Let's go back to the calculate function, but now we will add an overloaded function that allows you to calculate decimal values.

```
#include <iostream>

int calculate (int x, int y);
float calculate(float x, float y);
const int MAININT = 4;

int main()
{
   int result = calculate (5, 5);
    cout << result + MAININT;
    return 0;
}

int calculate(int x, int y)
{
        int result = x * y;
        return result;
}

float calculate(float x, float y)
{
        int result = x * y;
        return result;
}
```

When you add a function, don't forget to add its prototype. We added the prototype as well as a new calculate function. Notice that the calculate function has the same name, but it has a different data type and parameter list. The parameters are set as floating decimal point values, because we want to let our program calculate decimals as well as integers.

You might ask yourself how the program knows what function to call. Since we have a different data type and calling parameters, the compiler automatically knows what function to call by how you call the function. Let's use both functions in our program.

```cpp
#include <iostream>

int calculate (int x, int y);
float calculate(float x, float y);
const int MAININT = 4;

int main()
{
    int result = calculate (5, 5);
    float fresult = calculate (7.5, 7.5);
    cout << result + fresult;
    return 0;
}

int calculate(int x, int y)
{
        int result = x * y;
        return result;

}

float calculate(float x, float y)
{
        int result = x * y;
```

```
    return result;
}
```

Our program now calls the calculate function for integers and the calculate function for floating point decimals. We don't need to do anything specific with the calling statement, because the compiler already knows what function to call since we use decimals in one statement and integers in another. Just remember that the return values have different data types, so you need to make corresponding variables for the return results that match the return data type.

Functions are an integral part of any C++ program. You'll see them in any function, because the main foundation for a C++ language is the main function. When you overload your functions, ensure that it makes logical sense to use an overloaded function instead of a new function with a new name. This chapter gave you the starting concepts for your C++ programs, but it takes practice to fully understand the way functions work.

Lab Questions

1. When you create your function, what must you also do to ensure that the compiler doesn't give you an error?

a. set up a prototype statement
b. set the function as void
c. always return a value
d. remove any if statements

Explanation: the C++ language requires prototyping of functions, which means you must set the function definition at the beginning of your program files or the compiler gives you an error.

2. What method is used when you want to use the same function with different parameters?

a. encapsulation
b. overloading
c. dynamic variables
d. global variables

Explanation: Overloading a function means that the function has the same name, but different parameters and return types set the function apart.

3. When you define a variable in a function, what type of scope does it have?

a. global
b. local
c. overloaded
d. predefined

Explanation: a variable defined within a function has a local scope. When the function is finished executing, the variable is destroyed in memory.

4. When you don't want to return a value in a function, what data type should it use?

a. void
b. int
c. float
d. char

Explanation: the void data type tells the compiler that no value is returned from the function.

Chapter 9: Operator Overloading

Objective: This chapter teaches you how to overload common operators, which changes the way C++ works with standard arithmetic and assignment operators.

In previous chapters, we've seen the way C++ works with operators. When we assign a value to a variable, C++ uses the equal sign. When you want to add two numbers, you use the plus sign. We've seen several different operators, and each of them can be overloaded to function differently within your programs.

A Brief Overview of Operators

We've used operators in a very basic way. We assumed that the plus sign means to add two numbers. We assumed that the equal sign always assigns a value to a variable. In fact, operators act like functions in C++. We discussed functions and overloading functions in the last chapter, so you should have a strong idea of how functions work.

Let's take a look at a simple, standard line of code that adds two numbers.

```
int int1 = 1;
int int2 = 2;
int int3 = int1 + int2;
```

The obvious response to this code is that two variables were created, and those two variables are added together and assigned to a third variable.

We assume that the plus sign means addition, because that's what we're trained to understand from writing. However, the plus sign is actually a function in C++. Let's look at a visual example from what we know about functions.

```
int int1 = 1;
int int2 = 2;
int int3 = operator+(int1, int2);
```

The above code is a better representation of what happens when you use the plus operator. The system sends both integers to add in a function, the calculation is made, and then the result is assigned to the int3 variable.

The above code works with the arithmetic add function, but you can use this concept on any operator. If you remember from the chapter 8, functions can have the same name and still be valid in your code. The name remains the same, but the parameters and data type are different. This differentiates the function from other functions of the same name. We're going to show you how to overload the different operators you normally see in C++.

Some of these concepts use classes, but you can ignore the classes for now. We will get into classes in the next chapter.

Overloading Arithmetic Operators

In the above section, we showed you an example of the plus operator. We mentioned that the plus operator is actually a function named operator+(). The function takes two values and adds them both. However, you can also send two decimal numbers to the plus operator and yield the same type of result – the two values are added and the result is return. So what would you want to use the plus operator for if it performs what you want?

Perhaps you have your own data type and want to add a value within the structure. In most cases, you'll overload the operator within your own data types, especially classes. Classes are their own small component of a program, so they are also their own data type object. If you tried to add two custom data types together, the plus sign would fail. The compiler would not know what to do with the plus sign, so you'll receive an error from the program.

It's common for a C++ program to have its own data types that need to perform arithmetic functions. Let's use the Employee data type from previous chapters.

```
struct Employee
{
    int id;
    std::string firstname;
    std::string lastname;
    int birthyear;
};
```

To overload an arithmetic function, you use the friend function. The friend function takes the original function and uses it to overload your operator to a custom type of function. In this case, you want to add values within a specific structure. It's difficult to explain these overloads prior to looking at classes, so we'll create a small class. Just know that we'll explain classes in the next chapter, so you can reference the way classes are shown compared to how they work in the next chapter.

```
class Employee
{
private:
    int m_employeeId;
public:
```

```
Employee(int id) { m_employeeId = id; }

    friend Cents operator+(const Employee &c1, const
Employee &c2);

    int GetId() { return m_employeeId; }
};
Employee operator+(const Employee &c1, const Employee
&c2)
{
    return Employee (c1.m_ employeeId + c2.m_ employeeId);
}
```

The above code is a lot to take in when you haven't seen classes yet. Classes are their own object. This is an Employee class object. We decided to use this class object like the Employee structure data type we created earlier.

Let's take a look at what this class does. First, we create a class that contains an employee Id variable. We want to add employee Ids together in the class. We create an overloaded function that lets you pass two member Id variables to the class. Since these variables have their own data type of Employee, we need to overload the addition operator. We can't just add two Employee data types together.

The key to overloaded operators is the friend function. The friend function takes some of its parameters from the original addition function, and then amend the function to match our custom overloaded event. We need a function that will work with our Employee data type, so we've passed the friend function the address space for the passed parameters.

With our class created, we can now call the class and add two values. Let's take a look at the complete code.

```cpp
class Employee
{
private:
   int m_employeeId;
public:
   Employee(int id) { m_employeeId = id; }

   friend Cents operator+(const Employee &c1, const
Employee &c2);

   int GetId() { return m_employeeId; }
};
Employee operator+(const Employee &c1, const Employee
&c2)
{
   return Employee (c1.m_ employeeId + c2.m_ employeeId);
}

int main()
{
   Employee Emp1(6);
   Employee Emp2(8);
   Employee total = Emp1 + Emp2;
   std::cout << "I have " << total . GetId () << " total Ids." <<
std::endl;

   return 0;
}
```

As you can see, we still use the addition operator, but we add
to employee data type variables. Since we pass values directly
to the class constructor (we will learn constructors in the next
chapter), we can then add these two values in the overloaded
addition function.

We added the main function to perform the actual addition of your statements. All the rest of the main function is similar to what we've seen before.

We can do the same with the subtraction operator. Let's take a look at overloading the minus sign.

```cpp
class Employee
{
private:
    int m_employeeId;
public:
    Employee(int id) { m_employeeId = id; }

    friend Cents operator-(const Employee &c1, const Employee &c2);

    int GetId() { return m_employeeId; }
};
Employee operator-(const Employee &c1, const Employee &c2)
{
    return Employee (c1.m_ employeeId + c2.m_ employeeId);
}

int main()
{
    Employee Emp1(6);
    Employee Emp2(8);
    Employee total = Emp1 + Emp2;
    std::cout << "I have " << total . GetId () << " total Ids." << std::endl;

    return 0;
}
```

Notice that we only made one change – the operator function name was changed to operator-. We need to ensure that we change the right operator, and the minus sign uses the operator- function name. The above code subtracts Employee Ids.

You can also do the same with the multiplication and division operators as well as the modulus operator. Overloading operators isn't too common, but you will run into this technique in some C++ programs.

Overloading Comparison Operators

Once you know how to overload one set of operators, it's much easier to overload others. Comparison operators don't actually change a value. They just compare two values and respond with true or false.

Let's take a look at some sample code that compares employee ID numbers.

```
class Employee
{
private:
    double m_dX, m_dY, m_dZ;

public:
    Employee(double dX=0.0, double dY=0.0, double dZ=0.0)
    {
    m_dX = dX;
    m_dY = dY;
    m_dZ = dZ;
    }

    friend bool operator== (Employee &cP1, Employee &cP2);
    friend bool operator!= (Employee &cP1, Employee &cP2);
```

```
    double GetX() { return m_dX; }
    double GetY() { return m_dY; }
    double GetZ() { return m_dZ; }
};

bool operator== (Employee &cP1, Employee &cP2)
{
    return (cP1.m_dX == cP2.m_dX &&
        cP1.m_dY == cP2.m_dY &&
        cP1.m_dZ == cP2.m_dZ);
}
```

We've edited the Employee class to now use comparison overload functions. Notice that we still have the friend function. The friend function is the critical component for any operator overload function. In this example, we overload the == operator and the != operator. We allow the operator functions to compare our custom Employee class. Now let's take a look at the complete code with the main function calling the new overloaded functions.

```
class Employee
{
private:
    double m_dX, m_dY, m_dZ;

public:
    Employee(double dX=0.0, double dY=0.0, double dZ=0.0)
    {
    m_dX = dX;
    m_dY = dY;
    m_dZ = dZ;
    }

    friend bool operator== (Employee &cP1, Employee &cP2);
    friend bool operator!= (Employee &cP1, Employee &cP2);
```

```cpp
      double GetX() { return m_dX; }
      double GetY() { return m_dY; }
      double GetZ() { return m_dZ; }
};

bool operator== (Employee &cP1, Employee &cP2)
{
    return (cP1.m_dX == cP2.m_dX &&
        cP1.m_dY == cP2.m_dY &&
        cP1.m_dZ == cP2.m_dZ);
}
int main()
{
    Employee Emp1(6);
    Employee Emp2(8);
    Employee total = Emp1 != Emp2;
    std::cout << "I have " << total << " total Ids." << std::endl;

    return 0;
}
```

As you can see, this code is not much different than the code that overloads the arithmetic functions. We just need to assign the right overloaded function name. In this case, we wanted to overload comparison operators, so we used the operator== and operator!= functions. Again you'll see the friend function modifier. This modifier is necessary when overloading operators.

The rest of the code compares the two values that we send to the class functions and responds with true or false. Remember that the results or output variable that is returned from an overloaded function is still the same as the original function.

Overloading Increment and Decrement Operators

You'll recall from previous chapters that the increment and decrement operators add one or subtract one from a value. Both of these operators are useful for shorthand operations when you need to add or subtract 1 from a variable.

We've already seen overload operators for others, so this should start to get easier for you. Let's take a look at the code.

```
class Employee
{
private:
   int m_emp;
public:
   emp (int emp1=0)
   {
      m_ emp = emp1;
   }

   Employee & operator++();
   Employee & operator--();

   int GetDigit() const { return m_n emp Digit; }
};

Employee & Employee::operator++()
{
   if (m_ emp == 9)
      m_ emp = 0;

   else
      ++m_ emp;

   return *this;
}

Employee & Employee::operator--()
```

```
    {
        if (m_ emp == 0)
            m_ emp = 9;
        else
            --m_ emp;

        return *this;
    }
```

This class and its functions are much more complex, because we have to account for numbers that both decrement and increment. Notice that we don't need the friend function this time. We can create our own operator overloads without the friend function, because we don't need to account for any multiple value types. We just need to add or subtract 1 for any value passed to the overloaded function.

Let's take a look at the full code with the main function making a call to the overloaded function.

```
class Employee
{
private:
    int m_emp;
public:
    emp (int emp1=0)
    {
        m_ emp = emp1;
    }

    Employee & operator++();
    Employee & operator--();

    int GetDigit() const { return m_n emp Digit; }
};
```

```cpp
Employee & Employee::operator++()
{
  if (m_ emp == 9)
    m_ emp = 0;

  else
    ++m_ emp;

  return *this;
}

Employee & Employee::operator--()
{

  if (m_ emp == 0)
    m_ emp = 9;
  else
    --m_ emp;

  return *this;
}

int main()
{
    Employee Emp1(6);
    Employee Emp2(8);
    Employee total = Emp1++;
    std::cout << "I have " << total << " total Ids." << std::endl;

    return 0;
}
```

Just like the other overloaded functions, we again use the main function to call the class member functions to use the overloaded method.

We don't need the friend function type because we just need to increment a numeric value either by one or decrement a number by one.

Overloading operators is a common concept in some programs, but they aren't common. You should still understand the concepts and learn how you can make your own overloaded operators. This chapter helped you understand the basic concepts, so you can take them and use them in your own programs. Once you understand overloading, you can understand some important parts of C++ and object oriented programming.

Lab Questions

1. When you use a mathematical operator in your programs, what actually happens with the calculation is made?

a. the operation is actually a function operation
b. the function is removed from the computer's memory
c. the operation is calculated using outside libraries
d. the calculation is made differently

Explanation: operators look like simple mathematical operations in C++, but operators in C++ are actually functions.

2. What is the function operator you must use when you want to overload an operator in C++?

a. parent
b. friend
c. private
d. public

Explanation: the friend operator is needed when overloading arithmetic and comparison operators in C++.

3. When you pass variables to your overloaded function, how do you pass them?

a. using a pointer variable operator
b. using the variable's value
c. pass the entire custom class object
d. using the values memory address

Explanation: passing the memory address is the way to pass values to your custom class functions and overload the way a standard operator functions.

Chapter 10: Object Oriented Programming with C++

Objective: This chapter gives you an introduction to object-oriented programming (OOP). OOP is the foundation for programming reusable code, and it can be used in other languages.

Object-oriented programming (OOP) is what distinguishes C++ from its predecessor C. C is good for low-level programming, but OOP is necessary for large scale programs that power the web and internal applications. OOP is a more advanced subject, but you must know these principles to fully understand how to use the C++ language. We went into OOP a bit in the last chapter, but we're going to focus more on the topic in this chapter. This chapter is dedicated to OOP and its design principles.

A Brief Overview of OOP Design

Before going into OOP structures, it's important to understand the way OOP is designed to work with a program. The typical way to explain OOP is using a car. When you think of a car, you know that the car has parts. Each part is its own unique component, but the components come together to form a fully functional car.

Each component performs a function for the car. For instance, the engine enables the car to move. The steering wheel controls the direction, and the trunk lets you store content. All of these components perform actions.

The engine moves the car, the steering wheel turns left or right, and the trunk hatch can be opened and can store content. These actions are the "verbs" for an OOP program.

Components also have properties. These properties are the "nouns" in an OOP program. Properties describe the component. The engine is 8 liters, the trunk is black, and the steering while is black as well. These are properties of the object.

As you describe your car, you can get more and more detailed about its design. This same design can be used to describe a program. In OOP, the main object you program is called a class. A class would represent the components we just described for our car. Each class is designed with the idea that it forms a purpose for your application. Think of a CRM application. A class would represent a customer, an order, and even a product. Of course, you would have several classes and subclasses for a large application, but these OOP concepts help you design your software.

Classes are broken down into subclasses through inheritance. We'll cover inheritance in the next chapter. In the example of our car, the engine would be a class, the steering wheel would be another class and then the trunk would be a third class. These classes come together to form your car.

With the "verbs" or actions that the classes do, they are created in the form of methods. Methods are the actions your class does. For instance, you could have a method named "move" for the engine. Methods are just another way to say "function." The only difference between a method and a function is that a method is a part of a class where a function is a standalone subroutine.

Just get used to the terminology "method" when you see a discussion about function of a class. Methods are always the verbs, so they perform an action within the class.

Next are the properties. Properties are the nouns for the class, so they describe a class's features. For instance, the steering wheel is black, round, and has the air bag in the center. These are properties that describe the class, and you use these to build your class design. The trunk dimensions, whether or not it's empty or full and its color are also properties for the class. As you can see, you can get as detailed as you need for each class.

Once you put all of your component classes together, then you have a full car. The car in this analogy is the program. You classes can be used to build other programs, which is another benefit of writing modular code. For instance, you could use the same steering wheel class for another car, because the steering wheel is generally the same among all cars.

This is a brief overview of classes and OOP. Now we'll take a look at some code and more architecture samples.

Classes

We already saw some examples of classes, but we didn't go into details. Classes and structures are very similar, except classes provide you with more ability to create complete components rather than limit you to properties.

Let's use the Employee structure we created in earlier chapters and use it to create a class.

The original Employee structure looks like the following.

struct Employee

```
{
    int id;
    std::string firstname;
    std::string lastname;
    int birthyear;
};
```

Now let's turn this structure into a class.

```
class Employee
{
public:
    int id;
    std::string firstname;
    std::string lastname;
    int birthyear;
};
```

As you can see, not much difference between a class and a structure. The one main difference is that we specify that we are creating a class, and then we see the public modifier. The public modifier indicates that you want to make the class public to other sections of your program. You can also set your class as private, so no other classes could call it. For the most part, your classes will remain public.

Constructors and Destructors

Constructors and destructors are also important parts of classes. A constructor is what allows you to instantiate a class. You also need to make the class public to instantiate it from another part of your program, but constructors are the second part of the instantiation process.

Instantiation is what lets you create a class object in your program.

Without the constructor, you would not be able to dynamically create class objects. Let's use the Employee class to create a constructor for our class.

```
class Employee
{
public:
   Employee() { }
   int id;
   std::string firstname;
   std::string lastname;
   int birthyear;
};
```

We added the Employee constructor. This is a function that always has the same name as the class. You can overload the constructor just like you overloaded other functions. The overloaded constructor takes different types of parameters to differentiate it with other constructors. Let's add an overloaded constructor to see what it looks like.

```
class Employee
{
private:
   int m_id;
public:
   Employee() { }
   Employee(int id)
   {
      m_id = id;
   }
   int id;
   std::string firstname;
   std::string lastname;
   int birthyear;
};
```

We added a new constructor that takes a parameter named ID. You'll also note that we added a private section. This private section cannot be called by an outside class. Even if the class itself is public, the instantiated class can't see a private member. We created a private employee Id member variable named m_id. This is used to contain the employee's ID. Private members are typically those values that you don't want the instantiated class object to edit. Since an employee Id wouldn't change, you send the overloaded constructor the employee's Id and then store it in the private member Id variable. These variables are called properties as well. The variables you see in this defined class are all called properties – some are dynamic and some are private and static.

We're just missing a destructor from our class. A destructor does the opposite as the constructor. A destructor is what's called when you want to destroy the class. In other words, you want to remove it from memory. Destructors aren't technically called manually. The destructor is called when the program closes or the function goes out of scope. Destructors are important for removing unneeded code from memory.

First, let's add the destructor to the Employee class.

```
class Employee
{
private:
    int m_id;
public:
    Employee() { }
    Employee(int id)
    {
        m_id = id;
    }
    int id;
    std::string firstname;
```

```cpp
    std::string lastname;
    int birthyear;

    ~Employee()
    {
      m_id = 0;
    }
};
```

Notice that the constructor has a different structure than the constructor. The destructor always starts with the tilde (~) character. The destructor never has any parameters. You just use the destructor to clean up any variables you want to remove from memory. In this instance, we set the id to 0.

Let's first add a member function to the class, and then we'll see what happens when the destructor is called. Member functions are a part of the class, so the actions that they do should always match the class they are in. For instance, you wouldn't put a class that controls product in the Employee class. For instance, an Employee would clock time during the day. We could use a member function named ClockTime in the Employee class. Let's add this function to the class.

```cpp
class Employee
{
private:
    int m_id;
public:
    Employee() { }
    Employee(int id)
    {
        m_id = id;
    }
    int id;
```

```cpp
    std::string firstname;
    std::string lastname;
    int birthyear;

    void ClockTime()
    {
        // clocktime code goes here
    }

    ~Employee()
    {
      m_id = 0;
    }
};
```

We added a method that allows the employee to clock time.
This is our entire class object, so now we can use it in our
code. We'll call the class in the main function in our program.
Let's take a look at all of the code put together.

```cpp
class Employee
{
private:
    int m_id;
public:
    Employee() { }
    Employee(int id)
    {
        m_id = id;
    }
    int id;
    std::string firstname;
    std::string lastname;
    int birthyear;

    void ClockTime()
```

```
    {
        // clocktime code goes here
    }

    ~Employee()
    {
        m_id = 0;
    }
};

int main()
{
    Employee emp( 2 );
    std::cout << "The employee time clocked is  : " <<
emp.ClockTime() << std::endl;
    return 0;
} // The destructor is called here!
```

In the main function, we call a new variable. You'll see that we use the Employee data type since classes are their own custom data type. We then give the variable the name emp and we pass an employee Id to the calling function. We could pass the class no variable at all, and the first constructor would be called. Note that if there is no constructor, you can't instantiate a class, so ensure that your classes have constructors before you instantiate a variable.

We've decided to instantiate the employee with an Id of 2. After we instantiate the class, we can then use its member functions. The ClockTime member function doesn't do anything, but we call it in the cout call assumingly to print out the employee's time. What you create within the function is up to you. You are in control of the member class functions, and they should always perform an action on the Employee object.

Finally, return the integer value 0 to the main function. Once this main function ends, the Employee class destructor is called. Since the destructor changes the employee variable value to 0, the id is changed to zero and the class object is destroyed.

Turning Your Variables to Static

Static variables are also an option in your class objects. Static member variables work a little differently than regular variables. Static member variables act like global variables. If you remember from previous chapters, we discussed global versus local variables. In the last section, all of the class variables were local member variables that could not be accessed outside the class unless you specifically called them or returned them in your member functions.

With static member variables and functions, the value can be called even in other class objects in your code. In other words, the static member variable value remains the same regardless of what object you're using. Let's take a look at some example code, and we'll change our variable to static.

```
class Employee
{
private:
   int m_id;
public:
   Employee() { }
   Employee(int id)
   {
      id = id;
   }
   static  int id;
   std::string firstname;
   std::string lastname;
```

```cpp
    int birthyear;

    void ClockTime()
    {
        // clocktime code goes here
    }

    ~Employee()
    {
        m_id = 0;
    }
};

int main()
{
    Employee emp1 ( 2 );
    Employee emp2 ( );
    std::cout << "The employee time clocked is  : " << emp2.id
<< std::endl;
    return 0;
} // The destructor is called here!
```

In the above code, we changed the assignment to the Id
passed to the Employee constructor. It now points to a static
integer variable that's public, so we can call it from outside of
our class. Notice that we called the second constructor with no
parameters for emp2. This means that no value is set for the
employee's ID. However, we call the emp2.id property when
we print out the statement. The printout will be 2 even though
we never set the Id for the second Employee class object.

Static properties are useful when you need a variable to act
globally throughout several class objects as we used in this
example.

This chapter focused on the basics of classes. You'll need to practice as much as possible to understand how they work and what you can do with them when designing your applications. You should do your best to understand classes, because they are a part of most large scale applications especially if they are coded in the C++ language.

Lab Questions

1. When you want to make your class variables global, what modifier do you use?

a. global
b. const
c. private
d. static

Explanation: The static modifier turns local class variables into globally accessible variables regardless of the class that it's called from.

2. When you want to allow code to instantiate the class, what do you need to add?

a. destructor
b. constructor
c. member function
d. private members

Explanation: a constructor allows a class to be instantiated, and it can be used to set default values in a class object by overloading the default constructor.

3. You want to write a destructor for the Employee class. Write the proper syntax for the destructor.

~Employee() { }

Explanation: The destructor is always the same name as the class object. It always has the tilde prefix, and it never takes any parameters.

4. If you want to allow a class to be instantiated by external classes, aside from including a constructor, what do you need to do with the class?

a. set it to private
b. set it to public
c. make variables static
d. include a destructor

Explanation: A private class cannot be instantiated, but a public class can be instantiated from any other class in your program.

Chapter 11: Inheritance

Objective: this chapter teaches the programmer to inherit classes from parent classes to define reusable code throughout their program.

We discussed classes in the last chapter, and we focused on creating a class that described our Employee database. We used a car to describe the way classes are designed. We missed one part of class design – class inheritance. Inheritance allows you to derive information from a parent class and use it in the child class. This chapter discusses the way inheritance works and how you can design fully functional C++ programs by inheriting objects from your main parent class objects.

An Overview of Inheritance

Before we get into the code for inheritance, it's important to understand the basics. Inheritance lets you derive classes from parent classes. Imagine you want to create a program named Animal. You need to then describe several animals and their function.

Animals have some basic characteristics that they share across all species. Eyes, nose, and skin can be found on all animals. These characteristics can change in property, but you know that all animals have these three characteristics. The animal class could be the parent class for all of your animals.

Now, you know that cats and dogs are also animals. Cats have eyes, a nose and skin. Dogs also have skin, a nose and eyes.

Therefore, these two classes can derive their traits from the main animal class.

You can also have child of child classes. For instance, with your dog class, you could then have subclasses that describe different breeds of dogs. They are all dogs, so dogs would still remain as the parent class, but each breed would have its own characteristics, properties and methods. This chapter helps you understand the way inheritance works.

Basic Inheritance

Let's go back to the Employee class we worked with in the last chapter. We want to create a parent class for employees called Person. The parent class describes any employee, because all of our employees are people. However, you still need to describe employees, executives, owners, and vendors. All of these people could be their own class, and they would derive from the parent Person class since they are all a part of the person class.

Let's first look at the Employee class from the previous chapter.

```
class Employee
{
private:
   int m_id;
public:
   Employee() { }
   Employee(int id)
   {
      m_id = id;
   }
   int id;
```

```cpp
    void ClockTime()
    {
        // clocktime code goes here
    }

    ~Employee()
    {
        m_id = 0;
    }
};
```

Now we need to make a Person class. It could be very simple with just a few properties. For instance, every person has a name, so the firstname and lastname properties we used in the Employee class could be moved to the Person class. Let's do that and create a Person class in our code.

```cpp
#include <string>
class Person
{
public:
    std::string firstname;
    std::string lastname;
    int birthyear;

    std::string GetFirstName() { return firstname; }
    int GetBirthYeah() { return birthyear; }
    std::string GetLastName() { return lastname; }

    Person(std::string strName = "", int nAge = 0, bool bIsMale = false)
    {
    }
};
```

You'll notice that we have the same characteristics from our previous chapter. We have a public class named Person. The class has 3 member variables, which are the person's first and last name, and their birth year. We added three public member functions to get the first and last name and the birth year. Then, we added a constructor for the person's instantiation.

Now, we want the Employee class to derive from the person class. Let's take a look and see what we can do to the Employee class to derive members from the Person class.

```cpp
class Employee : public Person
{
private:
    int m_id;
public:
    Employee() { }
    Employee(int id)
    {
        m_id = id;
    }
    int id;


    void ClockTime()
    {
        // clocktime code goes here
    }

    ~Employee()
    {
        m_id = 0;
    }
};
```

If you take a look at the code, you'll see that there is only one small change to the code. The : public Person was added to the end of the class name. The colon character tells C++ that you want to derive or inherit from the parent class listed after the colon designation. When you derive from a parent class, that parent class properties and methods become available to the child class.

Now let's put the code together and look at the entire parent and child class objects together.

```cpp
#include <string>
class Person
{
public:
   std::string firstname;
   std::string lastname;
   int birthyear;

   std::string GetFirstName() { return firstname; }
   int GetBirthYeah() { return birthyear; }
   std::string GetLastName() { return lastname; }

   Person(std::string strName = "", int nAge = 0, bool bIsMale = false)
   {
   }
};


class Employee : public Person
{
private:
   int m_id;
public:
   Employee() { }
```

```cpp
    Employee(int id)
    {
        m_id = id;
    }
    int id;


    void ClockTime()
    {
        // clocktime code goes here
    }

    ~Employee()
    {
        m_id = 0;
    }
};
```

We now have a fully functional class and subclass structure.
With this new class structure, we can put our new code to the
test. We need to create some code that will work with the new
subclass and its parent. Remember that all parent class
methods and properties are available to the child class. This
means that we don't need to recreate the first and last name
properties in the Employee class. We already have these two
properties in the parent Person class. We can directly call the
first name and last name member variables and functions
from our Employee class. Let's take a look at an example.

```cpp
#include <string>
class Person
{
public:
    std::string firstname;
    std::string lastname;
    int birthyear;
```

```cpp
    std::string GetFirstName() { return firstname; }
    int GetBirthYeah() { return birthyear; }
    std::string GetLastName() { return lastname; }

    Person(std::string strName = "", int nAge = 0, bool bIsMale
= false)
    {
    }
};


class Employee : public Person
{
private:
    int m_id;
public:
    Employee() { }
    Employee(int id)
    {
        m_id = id;
    }
    int id;


    void ClockTime()
    {
        // clocktime code goes here
    }

    ~Employee()
    {
        m_id = 0;
    }
};

int main()
```

```
{
    Employee emp;
    emp.firstname = "John";
    std::cout << emp.GetFirstName() << std::endl;

    return 0;
}
```

We added the main function to call our Person and Employee class. First, we instantiate the Employee class and assign it to the emp variable. This variable automatically gets the Employee class properties and methods and it also gets the Person class since we derived from this class using inheritance.

Next, we give the employee a first name. We didn't define the first name in the Employee class, but we're still able to make a call to the firstname property since the class is inherited.

After we assign the name to the employee first name property, we then use the cout function to print the first name to the screen. Notice that this function isn't a part of the Employee class. It's also a part of the parent Person class. We can use both the property and the method without instantiating the Person class since we derived from it.

Controlling Derived Properties and Methods

Sometimes, you might not want some properties or methods to be derived from the parent class. You can change the way these features are derived using modifiers. The three modifiers we will cover are the public (which we already discussed), the private and protected keywords.

Let's say that we have a Person class and we want to set all Employees that we want to derive from the class to avoid changing critical information. For instance, we know that all people have eyes, so we want to always keep this value regardless of the derived class values. In other words, we want to "lock" some of the properties in the Person class.

Let's change two of our properties. We'll change one to protected and one to private and see how it changes the way the class derives and functions. Let's take a look at the two classes again.

```cpp
#include <string>
class Person
{
public:
    std::string firstname;
private:
    std::string lastname;
protected:
    int birthyear;

    std::string GetFirstName() { return firstname; }
    int GetBirthYeah() { return birthyear; }
    std::string GetLastName() { return lastname; }

    Person(std::string strName = "", int nAge = 0, bool bIsMale = false)
    {
    }
};


class Employee : public Person
{
private:
```

```cpp
    int m_id;
public:
    Employee() {}
    Employee(int id)
    {
        m_id = id;
    }
    int id;


    void ClockTime()
    {
        // clocktime code goes here
    }

    ~Employee()
    {
        m_id = 0;
    }
};
```

We now added the private and protected modifiers to the Parent class. We used private for lastname and protected for birthyear. We left the firstname public to demonstrate how all three modifiers work.

Now, let's use this code to understand what happens when you attempt to use the properties with these new modifiers added.

```cpp
#include <string>
class Person
{
public:
    std::string firstname;
private:
```

```cpp
    std::string lastname;
protected:
    int birthyear;

    std::string GetFirstName() { return firstname; }
    int GetBirthYeah() { return birthyear; }
    std::string GetLastName() { return lastname; }

    Person(std::string strName = "", int nAge = 0, bool bIsMale
= false)
    {
    }
};


class Employee : public Person
{
private:
    int m_id;
public:
    Employee() { }
    Employee(int id)
    {
        m_id = id;
    }
    int id;


    void ClockTime()
    {
        // clocktime code goes here
    }

    ~Employee()
    {
        m_id = 0;
```

```
        }
};

int main()
{
    Employee emp;
    emp.firstname = "John";
    emp.lastname = "Smith";
    emp.birthyear = 2000;
    std::cout << emp.GetFirstName() << std::endl;

    return 0;
}
```

We used the same basic code, but this time we added variable value assignments for all properties. This is what will happen to the code execution.

The first firstname property will execute successfully. The firstname property is set to public, and this allows any class to derive the properties and change their values.

The second property – lastname – is set to private. Private members cannot be accessed by derived classes. They are "private." A base class can access these members, which means any instantiation of the Person class is able to change the value of lastname, but our Employee class would be unable to change the firstname property, which means this assignment would fail in your code.

Next, we have the protected member, which is the birthdate property. Since we can derive protected members through inheritance, this assignment works as well. To wrap it up, the first and the third variables are derived and can be accessed by derived classes, but private members cannot.

Therefore, the second assignment of the lastname would fail, and your program would give the user an error.

These concepts will get you started with inheritance and object oriented programming. When you get several classes and subclasses, it can get confusing to keep track of the different parents and child classes, but you must be aware of when you can access different variables to avoid creating any errors in your program.

Lab Questions

1. To allow a child class to derive from a parent class, what is needed as the modifier for the main parent class?

a. public
b. private
c. any modifier will do
d. protected

Explanation: the public modifier allows any child class to derive from the parent class. It also allows outside functions instantiate the class for both the parent and the child.

2. You want to derive a child class called Dog from a parent class called Animal. Type the first line of code that defines the class and its inheritance.

class Dog : public Animal { }

Explanation: The Dog class derives from the parent Animal class by using a colon and then defining the parent class. The brackets are empty, but this is where you would place your class code including properties and methods.

3. When you derive a child class from a parent class and then want to use the parent class properties, what do you do?

a. instantiate the class and the use the properties from the derived child class
b. instantiate the parent class as well
c. call the parent class constructor
d. add a new function to call the parent class

Explanation: Derived child classes can use parent class properties as if they are a part of their own class.

Conclusion

This book has found you because you have the ultimate potential.

It may be easy to think and feel that you are limited but the truth is you are more than what you have assumed you are. We have been there. We have been in such a situation: when giving up or settling with what is comfortable feels like the best choice. Luckily, the heart which is the dwelling place for passion has told us otherwise.

It was in 2014 when our team was created. Our compass was this – the dream of coming up with books that can spread knowledge and education about programming. The goal was to reach as many people across the world. For them to learn how to program and in the process, find solutions, perform mathematical calculations, show graphics and images, process and store data and much more. Our whole journey to make such dream come true has been very pivotal in our individual lives. We believe that a dream shared becomes a reality.

We want you to be part of this journey, of this wonderful reality. We want to make learning programming easy and fun for you. In addition, we want to open your eyes to the truth that programming can be a start-off point for more beautiful things in your life.

Programming may have this usual stereotype of being too geeky and too stressful. We would like to tell you that nowadays, we enjoy this lifestyle: surf-program-read-write-eat. How amazing is that?

If you enjoy this kind of life, we assure you that nothing is impossible and that like us, you can also make programming a stepping stone to unlock your potential to solve problems, maximize solutions, and enjoy the life that you truly deserve.

This book has found you because you are at the brink of everything fantastic!

Thanks for reading!

You can be interested in: "C: Learn C In A DAY! - The Ultimate Crash Course to Learning the Basics of C In No Time"

Here is our full library: http://amzn.to/1HPABQI

To your success,
Acodemy.

57340051R00077

Made in the USA
Lexington, KY
13 November 2016